# Incorporating Pati
# in Japan and the U

MW00846072

Since the turn of the millennium, the potential for patients' knowledge to contribute to medical knowledge has been increasingly recognized by medical sociologists and anthropologists. Where previously such knowledge may have been written off as 'beliefs' and assumed to be inaccurate when it contradicted established medical science, it is increasingly recognized that patients—especially those with chronic conditions—can add a valuable perspective to the clinical knowledge of medical professionals. Sometimes this means working together to reassess treatment priorities, and at other times it may mean a patient-led movement to influence the direction of new research, based on patients' experiences.

Ushiyama takes the case of eczema (atopic dermatitis)— a chronic condition with a history of patient-led controversy over treatment methods—as a case study in how patient knowledge has come to affect change in medical practice. Comparing ethnographic fieldwork from Japan and the UK, she builds a complex picture of the differences in approach to treatment in light of attitudes to patients' knowledge.

**Miho Ushiyama** is a lecturer at the Department of Human Relations, Faculty of Human Relations, Otsuma Women's University, Japan.

# Routledge-WIAS Interdisciplinary Studies

*Edited by Hideaki Miyajima and Kazuhisa Takemura, Waseda University, Japan*

For the full list of book, please visit https://www.routledge.com/Routledge-WIAS-Interdisciplinary-Studies/book-series/WIAS01

# Incorporating Patient Knowledge in Japan and the UK

## A study of Eczema and the Steroid Controversy

**Miho Ushiyama**

Routledge
Taylor & Francis Group

LONDON AND NEW YORK

WiAS 早稲田大学高等研究所
Waseda Institute for Advanced Study

First published 2020
by Routledge
2 Park Square, Milton Park, Abingdon, Oxon OX14 4RN

and by Routledge
52 Vanderbilt Avenue, New York, NY 10017

*Routledge is an imprint of the Taylor & Francis Group, an informa business*

First issued in paperback 2021

*British Library Cataloguing-in-Publication Data*
A catalogue record for this book is available from the British Library

*Library of Congress Cataloging-in-Publication Data*
A catalog record for this book has been requested

ISBN: 978-1-138-33907-1 (hbk)
ISBN: 978-1-03-209005-4 (pbk)
ISBN: 978-0-429-44130-1 (ebk)

Typeset in Galliard
by codeMantra

To Matthew, Aki and Kazu

# Contents

# List of figures

# List of tables

# Preface

This book is a revised and extended version of my Japanese book, which was published by Shinyōsha in 2015, titled *Steroid to 'Kanjya no Chi': Atopīseihifuen no Ethnography (Steroids and 'Patient Knowledge': An Ethnography of Atopic Dermatitis)*.

The original reason I began investigating atopic dermatitis was simply because I also suffer from the disease, but as I delved further into it, I began to notice much deeper, far-reaching issues, including the conflict between doctors and patients surrounding treatment, problems concerning legitimacy in health care, and problems specific to Japan that become apparent when making comparisons with the UK. My outlook expanded the more I investigated, and this was one of the most rewarding aspects of completing this research.

This book looks at the problem of topical steroid side effects from the perspective of atopic dermatitis patients with particularly serious cases of the disease. Many atopic dermatitis patients have mild symptoms, so some readers may feel that there is some bias in the way the problems are presented in this book. However, a lot of research ultimately contains the author's subjectivity no matter how hard he or she may try to eliminate it. This book also reflects my personal experiences as someone who stopped using topical steroids, endured a relatively severe relapse, and eventually saw an improvement in my symptoms. If my symptoms had become unstable after discontinuing topical steroids, or if continuing to use topical steroids had allowed me to control my symptoms, I am sure this book would have been written very differently.

During the writing of this book, the situation of atopic dermatitis patients in English-speaking countries significantly changed. One of the main focuses of this book is an examination of the reasons why steroid withdrawal treatment, that is, stopping the use of steroids in order to cure atopic dermatitis, appeared in Japan but not in the UK, and this question was based on the fact that there was no steroid withdrawal treatment in the UK when I conducted fieldwork there between 2009 and 2012. However, after I left the UK, the situation changed, and steroid withdrawal treatment spread in the UK, like it has in other English-speaking countries. This trend started after the 2012 establishment of the International Topical Steroid Addiction Network (ITSAN) in the United States. ITSAN raises awareness of Red Skin Syndrome (RSS), which is another name for steroid withdrawal symptoms, and supports patients who withdraw from steroids. After this group was established, many patients in English-speaking countries started to become aware of the problems of RSS and steroid addiction and withdrawal, and the idea of steroid withdrawal treatment began to spread via social media, such as on blogs and Facebook.

Because steroid withdrawal treatment was not yet known in the UK when I conducted fieldwork there between 2009 and 2012, I assumed that steroid withdrawal treatment would be unlikely to spread in the UK while I was writing the manuscript of this book. However, the idea of steroid withdrawal treatment spread quickly through social media from 2012, and the situation in English-speaking countries became similar to that of Japan in the 1990s, when steroid withdrawal first started to spread there. This book thus illustrates the situation in the UK before steroid withdrawal treatment had spread and the situation in Japan after this treatment had spread. Some of my analysis might therefore be outdated when this book is published, but this is due to the rapidly changing situation in English-speaking countries.

# Acknowledgements

I started my research when I was a doctoral student of Waseda University in Japan, and continued my research when I moved to the UK to learn medical anthropology as a master's student in University College London. I greatly appreciate the professors and students I met there for their extensive comments and advice.

I also appreciate the Waseda Institute for Advanced Study (WIAS), where I was a research associate from 2013 to 2016, for offering me an opportunity to publish this book. This book could not have been published without the help of James Kirk, who translated my Japanese manuscript into English very accurately, and of Nick Kasparek, who copyedited the manuscript into sophisticated academic English.

Junko Kitanaka gave me invaluable support throughout the process of publishing this book. I am also indebted to her students for their stimulating arguments over my manuscript. Emma Cook kindly read my proposal for this book and gave me invaluable advice. I am also grateful to Takuya Matsushige, Daisuke Son, Jinpei Misawa, and Yōsuke Hatakeyama for their thoughtful comments.

In conducting the research for this book, I received funding from the following institutions: Waseda University, University College London, The Gushinkai Foundation, The Toyota Foundation, The Shibusawa Foundation for Ethnological Studies, and the Japanese Ministry of Education, Culture, Sports, Science and Technology. I would like to use this opportunity to express my gratitude.

During my research for this book, I was also able to meet many different patients and doctors by participating in the activities of the self-help group Atopy-free.com, the authorized NPO Atopicco Network for Children of the Earth, and the National Eczema Society. This research owes a great deal to these groups and their daily effort in helping to enrich people's social networks. I would like to express my thanks to them once again. I am also deeply thankful to all of the patients and doctors who agreed to participate in interviews that, at times, lasted over an hour.

I would like to thank my parents, Yukio and Mari Ushiyama, and my brother, Takayuki Ushiyama, for their support throughout all my research. Last but not least, I dedicate this book to my husband, Matthew Hanrahan, who has always supported me with his warm love, and to my daughter, Aki, and my son, Kazu.

# 1   Introduction

## The problem of steroids

> It hurt so much I could barely breathe. I wondered what I was living for. My whole body hurt yet felt numb. I couldn't move my hands, but I couldn't sleep either. The pain was too bad. Eating by myself was also too hard. I had to have food put into my mouth for me. I couldn't even open my eyes, so I couldn't watch TV. It was just kind of like counting from one to a hundred over and over. I'd scratch like crazy for about 12 hours, and then suffer terrible pain for another 12 hours. There was no chance to sleep. It was horrible. It hurt even to cry. There was no way I could cry, but my mother cried when she looked at me. I couldn't see it myself, but it seemed like I was all swollen up and in a horrible state. I first had a relapse when I was 24, and I looked absolutely awful. When my mother first saw me—she'd just got home—she screamed so loud I thought I must be dead. She wiped the cuts around my eyes while she cried and told me about the state I was in. All the while I was wondering if I was still alive or not.
>
> (Asami, 28, female)

These are the words of a 28-year-old atopic dermatitis[1] patient, Asami, describing how precipitously her condition had declined. While atopic dermatitis tends to be regarded as a light form of eczema, this disease has the potential to lead to desperate cases like Asami's. Such severe symptoms, however, only manifest under specific circumstances such as when patients stop using topical steroids. Topical steroids are a synthetic equivalent of corticosteroids, a class of steroid hormones involved in the regulation of inflammation,[2] that can be rubbed directly onto the skin. Steroid medication can also be ingested as tablets; but in this text, the term *steroids* will be used to refer to topical steroids unless otherwise stated. There is not yet a cure for atopic dermatitis, so general clinics and hospitals cannot address the root cause of the disease and can only provide treatment for its symptoms. In the case of atopic dermatitis, symptomatic treatment primarily involves the use of topical steroids, and when topical steroids are discontinued after a long period of use, patients can experience a relapse, which is known as a 'rebound' or 'withdrawal' among patients. This relapse can lead to symptoms as severe as those suffered by Asami. Yet, even after Asami herself learnt about this, she nonetheless chose to discontinue treatment, and went on to face the ordeal she described. What, then, motivated her to take such a risk and discontinue treatment?

Topical steroids were first used to treat atopic dermatitis in 1952 by dermatologist Dr. Marion B. Sulzberger; he was the first to use them for skin diseases generally, and he reported their effectiveness in the treatment of atopic dermatitis. In Japan, steroid medication was approved by the Ministry of Health and Welfare (now the Ministry of Health, Labour and Welfare) the following year, and it soon began to be used in treatment. When steroids first began to emerge, people were greatly impressed by their near-miraculous results and started to abuse them with little awareness of their side effects. There were women in Japan who even used steroids as a make-up primer after hearing that they made it easier to apply cosmetics. People soon learnt, however, that continued use of steroids gradually leads to symptoms such as skin atrophy and thinning, hair growth and red facial rashes, including rosacea-like dermatitis. The Japanese media focused on steroids in the 1990s, leading to information campaigns about the horrors of steroids. At the same time, patients were discovering that steroids become less effective the more they are used, and cases of relapses like Asami's grew more prevalent as more people stopped using them. This culminated in a significant avoidance of steroids and a so-called steroid phobia. From the 1980s into the 1990s, as the steroid phobia was spreading, a number of alternative Japanese therapies began appearing. These therapies claimed to cure atopic dermatitis and involved withdrawing from steroid medication. Companies targeting atopic dermatitis patients became so successful that they inspired the coining of a new term: *Atopy Business* (Takehara, 2000).

Asami sought out one such alternative therapy and was told that her atopic dermatitis would be cured if she stopped using steroids. She followed this advice and was soon enduring the ordeal she described. What this book aims to question is whether this stance against using steroids is unscientific, or if it is simply a respectable patient choice. Over the past few decades, the concept of what it means to be a patient has changed significantly. The idea of *patient knowledge*— that is, the knowledge patients have—has garnered a great deal of attention over this period and has been a key factor in driving change. This contrasts with how the professional knowledge of doctors has long been seen as the only legitimate source of knowledge. The doctor–patient relationship has been defined by a paternalistic model in which the patient blindly follows the authority of the doctor, with the patient's treatment dictated solely by the doctor's professional knowledge. With the increase in patients suffering from chronic diseases, conditions that cannot be cured by medical science have gradually come to dominate health care. The experience of these patients themselves has thus taken increasing importance. This has led to the view that patient knowledge should be valued even if it differs from professional knowledge.

The most significant challenges to respecting patient knowledge arise from the disconnects between the treatments patients desire and the treatments doctors provide. Whether patients' wishes should be privileged or whether doctors' professional knowledge should fundamentally determine treatment remains a source of conflict for those who support the idea of patient knowledge, and it could be said that the problems surrounding steroids are at the centre of this conflict. Should the opinions of patients who wish to discontinue steroids be respected, or should patients follow their doctor's guidance despite their fears? Depending on the viewpoint taken, choices like Asami's may be seen as unscientific and misguided or as reasonable and worthy of respect.

Whether the fear of steroids is scientifically valid or not remains unclear. Patients often come to mistrust steroids after long-term use because of medication no longer having clear effects or because of concerns about their long-term side effects. When patients suddenly discontinue steroids, however, many experience relapse. Some experience relapses so severe that they cannot attend school or work and find themselves isolated from society. After enduring such a relapse, which may last months or even years, many patients do experience some relief from their symptoms, but there is no guarantee of this.

Meanwhile, there is still no conclusive data on the long-term effects of steroid use. In severe cases of atopic dermatitis, patients must continue using steroids for decades, yet the longest clinical trial[3] or investigation I could find that focused on their side effects spanned only one year (Luger et al., 2004). Patients thus have no long-term data to consult regarding what they intently want to know: what exactly happens if one continues using steroids for decades? The current situation thus makes it difficult to judge if fearing steroids is irrational and mistaken or logical and valid. However, such dualistic thinking—positioning steroids as either dangerous or safe—traps patients in perpetual confusion. It is precisely the lack of hard data or evidence that impels patients to seek solace in clear and confident claims.

With no definitive answers available, this book aims to explore the range of views to which patients are exposed. I conducted investigations in Japan and the UK and examined the differing positions taken by modern medicine, alternative medicine, and self-help groups in both countries, as well as the effects of these views on patients in their respective cultures.

## The changing doctor–patient relationship

### *The doctor–patient relationship*

This book's investigation builds on an understanding of the history of the doctor–patient relationship and how ideas about patient knowledge have developed. In the treatment of atopic dermatitis, patients who resist using topical steroids are seen as problematic by doctors, and underlying this attitude is the implicit understanding that patients should follow their doctor's orders.

This view is based on a paternalistic model of the doctor–patient relationship in which the doctor's authority is unquestioned. In this model, the doctor is the expert in charge, and the patient's role is simply to do what the doctor says.

The history of this paternalistic model in modern medicine is an interesting one. In fact, the unquestioned authority of doctors is relatively recent, emerging with modern medicine's rise in the 19th century. Prior to this, doctors did not necessarily hold a strong position over patients and could even be seen showing remarkable humility (Kodama, 1998).

Yoshihito Kodama (1998) researched medical treatment in medieval Italy and found that in both Western Europe and Japan, the profession of 'doctor' was originally a humble one. It was not until universities and medical education were established that the current image of the all-powerful doctor came about, which in Japan was from the Meiji period onwards. Roy Porter's (1989) research on 18th-century quacks similarly showed that the power balance between patients and legitimate health care workers favoured the patient. Doctors at that time had little social standing and did not yet have any kind of professional association, so they had to endear themselves to their upper-class clientele for their pay, power, and status. Since they struggled to diagnose illnesses in an age that had no stethoscopes, X-rays, or laboratories, it was necessary for them to listen very carefully to what their patients said. In other words, the doctor–patient relationship required doctors to be good listeners and to respond to their patient's every need. Porter (1989) explains that doctors in those days were expected to act on their patient's orders, essentially serving to follow their patient's whims.

Doctors became an authoritative presence only from the 19th century, when modern medicine established itself and doctors secured their status as professionals. Medical sociologist Eliot Freidson uses the framework of professional dominance to explain how doctors have attained their authority. Freidson claims that doctors have gained their position not through individual abilities or interpersonal trust, but through securing legal status as experts. Three of Freidson's arguments are of particular relevance to understanding why doctors were able to gain their authoritative power.

Firstly, when the position of doctor became officially recognized as a profession, those without qualifications were no longer able to practise medicine, and doctors gained the exclusive right to provide medical services. Patients have since found it necessary to seek the advice of doctors whether they want to or not.

Secondly, since patients cannot procure vital materials or services without going through a doctor, doctors can be seen as holding power over them. Even if patients know the specific medicine they need, they cannot gain access to it without a doctor's prescription. When doctors possess exclusive access rights to the materials patients require, patients must obey doctors.

Thirdly, by limiting their number, doctors are able to maintain their position of strength and avoid having to obey patient demands. If the number of doctors were to increase, clients might themselves become licensed and organize to get what they want. The authority of doctors would then be greatly diminished. By keeping their numbers small relative to demand, and by preventing patients from creating any kind of organization, doctors can thereby protect their position of authority (Freidson, 1970).

Freidson's arguments explain well just how authoritative a position doctors were able to build for themselves by monopolizing medical treatment as a professional organization. However, this model of health care with absolute doctoral authority is now declining, with a model centred on patients beginning to form in its place. There are three key factors that help to explain the reasons behind this change.

The first factor is a change in the composition of diseases in society, that is, the relative prevalence of different types of diseases. In Japan, the top three causes of death between 1920 and 1950 were the infectious diseases pneumonia, gastroenteritis, and tuberculosis. However, in 1951, the top cause of death became cerebrovascular disease, and by 1960, all of the top three causes of death had become chronic diseases, namely, malignant neoplasms, heart disease, and cerebrovascular disease. Essentially, in the time between 1950 and 1960, there was a transition from an era of infectious diseases to an era of chronic diseases (or lifestyle diseases). Historian of science Yōichirō Murakami (2002) explains that during the infectious disease era, the medical care system could still function effectively despite an asymmetric doctor–patient relationship, since the treatment of infectious diseases requires very little involvement from the patient. Patients can simply have their infections cured by doctors, who eliminate pathogens through treatments such as intravenous drips, injections, or drug therapy. All of these treatments fall well within the discretionary powers of the doctor. Chronic diseases, on the other hand, cannot be completely cured like this, and so patients must learn to live with these diseases for their entire lives. Even if chronically ill patients do take medication, they will most likely have to continue taking it indefinitely, and the decision to do so rests entirely with the individual. As a result, the role of the patient in treating chronic diseases is of central importance. Even though the discretionary powers remain with the doctor, it is the patient who must carry them out; thus, the role of the patient has gained a great deal of attention (Murakami, 2002).

The second factor is the information technology revolution, which allowed for the digitalisation of scientific journals. Academic journals were once only intended to be read by professionals who registered and paid a membership fee; however, now even ordinary patients are able to access this knowledge online. As a result, while doctors' professional knowledge was once vastly superior to that of patients, it has become possible for patients to gain a high level of expertise on their own diseases.

The third factor is the increase from the 20th-century onwards of alternative medical treatments, that is, treatments other than those provided by modern medicine in Japan or in the West. With the rise of alternative medicine, patients have gained rights as consumers to select and pay for the kinds of treatment they want. Bonnie O'Connor (1995) has presented a model of patients as clients in which they gain this right to choose and, ironically, thereby claim a position of greater power.

These three factors have developed simultaneously, presenting a serious challenge to the hegemony of modern medicine and the paternalistic model of the doctor–patient relationship, which has greatly weakened the authority of doctors.

### The focus on illness narratives

As the authority of doctors has weakened, patient narratives have garnered increasing attention. In particular, there has been greater recognition that the experiences and stories of patients are especially meaningful regarding chronic diseases, which patients must often live with and control for their entire life.

Medical anthropologist Arthur Kleinman's work has been influential in inspiring this increased attention to patient narratives. In his book *The Illness Narratives: Suffering, Healing, and the Human Condition*, Kleinman (1988) warned that health care at present is completely devoted to the treatment of 'disease,' and so misses sight of the 'illness' that affects the patient and his or her family.

Disease, Kleinman argues, is a problem from the perspective of the healer, and this defines health in terms of medical classifications. Suppose, for example, a woman complains of chest pain. Using the definition of disease to treat her, the healer might give a diagnosis of coronary arterial disease and prescribe calcium channel blockers and nitroglycerin. However, this treatment would fail to consider various factors of the illness such as the woman's fear, the despair of her family, or its impact on her job.

By using the word *illness*, Kleinman shows that the experience of suffering is not reduced simply to a disease, but is expressed as a deeper social, cultural, and personal experience. What *illness* connotes is the experience of many interweaving factors, including how the people in a social network recognize and react to the illness, what kind of meaning the illness is given in a particular culture, and the experience of individuals themselves. Kleinman claims that in order for doctors to shift their focus to the illness, they must first listen carefully to the patient's narrative and then interpret and empathize with what they hear.

Kleinman's view is harshly critical of modern medicine, and he advocates a new and different form of treatment. As part of modern medical education, medical students study specialist skills exhaustively under the premise that all people are the same. In this form of education, asking about the patient's medical history is of secondary importance. However, as mentioned previously, in health care prior to the dawn of modern medicine, doctors needed to listen intently to the patient's narrative. In that era, how the patient described his or her medical history had a dramatic effect on their diagnosis. Furthermore, by listening to patients' narratives, doctors could sympathize with their anguish and attempt to soothe their illness, which was a crucial aspect of health care. Indeed, it was once common for doctors to write very personal clinical case studies, but after that practice peaked in the 19th century, it began to decline with the arrival of impersonal science-based thinking.

Perhaps the aim of Kleinman's illness narratives is to bring back to health care the soothing techniques used prior to medical science, which involved treating the patient as an individual human being, listening closely to his or her narrative, and providing an interpretation of the illness. In this way of thinking, the narrative of the patient's experience is far from meaningless; rather, it is a crucial factor in the provision of treatment.

Parallels with viewpoints like Kleinman's, in which emphasis is put on the patient narrative, can be seen in the concept of narrative-based medicine (NBM) proposed by Tricia Greenhalgh and Brian Hurwitz. NBM is a concept that came about by encouraging reflection on, and attempting to provide a complement to, evidence-based medicine (EBM), which is currently seen as the superior approach. Put simply, NBM means not focusing solely on scientific evidence in clinical settings, but placing importance also on respecting and interpreting the stories patients have to tell (Greenhalgh and Hurwitz, 1998). The use of NBM has gained support in various nursing and health care settings, and the approach of listening carefully to patient narratives is gradually permeating the clinical world too. NBM's growing popularity has started influencing the way health care workers view patients. Indeed, this area of research is one of the driving forces behind the increasing respect for patient experiences and narratives.

## Patient knowledge

While patient narratives have become a central research topic in medical anthropology, research into patient knowledge has mostly been limited to scientific studies. Even until around the 2000s, medical anthropology and medical sociology mostly described patients' understandings as 'lay beliefs,' as clearly distinct from 'professional knowledge.' Using the term 'belief' implies that lay people have irrational or scientifically wrong ideas and that these should be replaced by the correct 'knowledge' of professionals (Good, 1994). However, the boundary between lay and professional ways of thinking has blurred in recent years, and researchers have started to refer to lay ways of thinking, not as 'beliefs' but as 'knowledge.'

One of the reasons for this change has been the relative increase in chronic illnesses and the fact that patients' experiences and knowledge play a more important role in treatments than previously acknowledged. Exemplifying this shift, the Department of Health in the UK introduced the concept of 'expert patients' in the National Health Service (NHS) in 1999 in response to the increasing number of patients with chronic illnesses. These expert patients were then expected to take an active role in their own care by using their own skills and knowledge, since they were assumed to have expertise based on their experience of living with illness (Department of Health, 2001).

The shift from belief to knowledge has also been driven by the emergence of movements in which patients actually produce medical knowledge (Epstein, 1996; Callon and Rabeharisoa, 2003). While it was long assumed that most medical knowledge is produced by professionals, this is no longer taken for granted. Underlying this trend has been the rise of research that questions the accepted orthodoxy of science and medical knowledge. Some of this research has emerged from an academic field that started in the 1970s and includes the strong programme, laboratory studies, the sociology of scientific knowledge (SSK), and science, technology and society (STS). Research in this field has elucidated the political and social structure of science long accepted simply as self-evident knowledge. Bruno Latour's *Science in Action: How to Follow Scientists and Engineers through Society* provides an example of this. Latour explains that scientific knowledge is not just a collection of indisputable facts, but is instead something shaped by the scientists who are able to win the most arguments. The very nature of science, even as the foundation of the knowledge base with the greatest legitimacy, is thus increasingly being recognized as something constructed rather than as an established source of facts beyond dispute (Latour, 1987). In turn, this brings into question the correctness of treatments carried out by health care professionals based on the legitimacy of science and existing health care. In this context, patient experience and knowledge can begin to cast doubt on and challenge the professional knowledge of doctors.

## Patient involvement in medical research

Medical knowledge production by patients is primarily through their involvement in medical research practices (Epstein, 1996; Callon and Rabeharisoa, 2003). The classic case of such involvement is Steven Epstein's report on HIV/AIDS activists. He carried out research on AIDS treatment activism and detailed how activists were able to gain credibility both in society and among experts, and then go on to change the way the knowledge of medical science was formed.

The activists were AIDS or HIV patients who, even when AIDS treatment was approaching the stage of clinical trials, would simply be left with the fate of dying from the disease unless they happened to be part of the trials and had a chance to try the drugs. This was because in order for drugs to be approved in the United States, they first had to pass three stages of clinical trials that demonstrated the safety and efficacy of the drug. This process typically required six to eight years. The activists got to work to change this system, realising that a large number of patients could die while waiting for the approval of a drug. They first studied the language and culture of medical science, eventually reaching a level of knowledge that allowed them to argue at an expert level. By employing the terminology and concepts of virology, immunology, and biostatistics, they obliged experts to engage with their arguments.

The activists also changed the way clinical trials were carried out. Since joining a clinical trial and taking the new drug meant the chance of a prolonged life, activists believed that AIDS or HIV patients should share this opportunity equally. Up to that point, trial participants had typically been middle-class white men, but the activists claimed that the real world was far more diverse and that this diversity should be reflected in trials. As a result, it became possible for a wide range of people to participate in the trials, including male and female, white and non-white, and straight and gay.

Moreover, before then, people who were taking other drugs or who had taken them in the past were prevented from joining trials, since this seemed to make collecting clean data easier. As a result, only people who had never taken drugs could join trials, and people never had more than a single chance to join. This led to people lying, however, and unnecessarily jeopardized the accuracy of the data. The activists claimed that rather than focusing on collecting clean and perfect data, the trials should reflect the reality of how a large number of people actually live, that is, by taking various kinds of drugs.

The efforts of the activists became even more wide-ranging, and they reached such a level of expertise that there was little to differentiate them from the established experts. Their arguments were published in scientific journals; they attended official scientific conferences; and their opinions and review committee had a strong influence on decisions regarding what research would receive funding. Furthermore, they contributed heavily to forming new drug regulation mechanisms by making drugs more accessible and increasing rates of approval, among other achievements.

It could be said that what the activists achieved upended how scientific medical knowledge had previously been formed. Territory only accessible by experts was now being encroached upon by patients, and even within scientific debate, the opinions of laypeople began to have an impact on outcomes. AIDS activists also inspired activism in other areas of medicine, including cancer treatment, and they forged a template for patients to involve themselves in the medical world.

Patient involvement in medical research has since been reported in the fields of cancer research generally (Hess, 1999) and breast cancer research specifically (Brown, 2007; Klawiter, 2008; Ley, 2009; McCormic, 2009), as well as research on rare diseases (Panofsky, 2011), mental illnesses (Crossley, 2006), and Alzheimer's disease (O'Donovan et al., 2013).

In the UK, patient involvement in medical research has even been established at the national level. The Department of Health established a system of patient and public involvement (PPI) in 1996 (its name changed to INVOLVE in 2003), in which patients are involved not as research subjects but as active participants in research. The rationale for this practice is the recognition that lay experiential knowledge is a valid form of evidence and all stages of the medical research process can benefit from involving patients (McKevitt, 2013).

## Contested illnesses

While many cases of patient involvement in medical research look successful in terms of cooperation between patients and scientists, cases of 'contested illnesses' show the difficulty of filling the gap between patient knowledge and the existing medical knowledge produced by scientists. The notion of contested illnesses highlights issues involving scientific uncertainty and contestation, such as toxic exposure, Gulf War–related illnesses, environmental breast cancer, asthma, and chronic fatigue syndrome. Laypeople have challenged the existing medical knowledge regarding the definitions, causes, treatments, and prevention of these diseases, often with the support of academic researchers. The movements behind such challenges are termed 'health social movements' (Brown et al., 2011), and they have demonstrated that scientific knowledge is co-produced by governments, industries, community advocates, and academic researchers.

However, with contested illnesses, it is not always the case that laypeoples' claims about diseases are fully accepted and legitimized by governments, academia, and the public at large. Hilary Arksey's work on repetitive strain injury (RSI) illustrates this ambivalence. RSI is a condition that can appear in areas such as the hands, wrists, neck, or shoulders, and it is believed to be caused by a static working posture, repetitive actions, and psychological stress. What is of particular interest about this condition is the debate among patients, doctors, specialists, academics, and the media surrounding whether or not it even exists. In fact, since RSI is not something with a visual manifestation, it would go completely unnoticed if not for patients' complaints.

RSI organizations claim that the condition is caused by occupational factors, and aim to have this broadly recognized by society. Doctors, on the other hand, question this assertion by indicating other issues such as patient anxiety or by suggesting that patients may insist on having a condition just to receive payouts.

Arksey's explanation of the process of how RSI became established as a disease, from the perspective of both patients and doctors, leads to a remarkable set of observations: If the existence of RSI were to be confirmed as a scientific fact, this would open the possibility of patients influencing the formation of medical knowledge. However, those in such a position of weakness as patients can only succeed in confirming new medical knowledge if they work alongside professionals. Arksey's observations highlight the paradox of patient knowledge having great potential to contribute to establishing new medical facts, but, at the same time, patients being unable to evoke change in medical knowledge without the support of professionals (Arksey, 1998).

Medical sociologist Takuya Matsushige's research on patient-centred medicine also provides intriguing insights into patient knowledge. Matsushige draws on the example of the MMR vaccine controversy in the UK and explains what happens when the professional knowledge of doctors and scientists clashes with the knowledge of patients and their families. The MMR vaccine is an immunization vaccine which protects against measles, mumps, and rubella. In 1998, Andrew Jeremy Wakefield's research team reported 12 instances of autism in patients who had received the MMR vaccine and concluded that it was possible that the vaccine had induced autism. This conclusion developed into a controversy involving members of the general public. However, there was no solid evidence to support this argument, and nothing conclusive was ever brought forward. Parents of young children, meanwhile, demanded selective vaccines be used for each disease, rather than a combined vaccine for all three. Health care authority experts, on the other hand, emphasized the safety of the MMR vaccine and rejected the parents' opinions. Matsushige (2010: 3) summarizes the argument surrounding the MMR vaccine as follows:

> This controversy centres around the idea of what constitutes medically sound information. In other words, in the expert–amateur equation, since only the information deemed 'correct' by the former (scientists and doctors) is pursued, any opportunity to consider how the latter (in this case, the

parents) logically form judgements about what is valuable is disregarded. The result is that the claims of the parents are characterized as unscientific, misperceptions, or mistaken facts, and receive no other interpretation.

In this case, by labelling patients' views as 'unscientific, misperceived, or mistaken facts,' and portraying the experts' opinions as the one true source of medical knowledge, health care authorities foreclosed any possibility of a compromise with the concerned public. In Arksey's example of RSI organizations, by working together with experts, patients were able to influence the formation of new medical knowledge, but the MMR vaccine example shows us that patient knowledge can also be silenced by expert opinion.

If the three discussed examples of patient knowledge regarding the formation of medical knowledge are considered alongside each other, a recurring characteristic becomes evident. With the RSI recognition movement Arskey examined, the MMR vaccine controversy Matsushige discussed, and the AIDS activism Epstein depicted, the opinions of the patients and their families were evaluated strictly in terms of how scientific they were deemed to be by the experts involved.

In the case of the MMR vaccine controversy, since the parents' opinions had no scientific validity, they were deemed unscientific and thus disregarded by the experts. In the case of RSI, patients worked together with experts and found that carrying out the debate on a scientific level was a prerequisite for them to gain any legitimacy. In the case of AIDS, since the activists acquired a level of scientific knowledge that put them on equal terms with the experts, they were able to break into the world of medical science and assert their influence. In every case, it seems that in order for patients to attain medical legitimacy, they must engage experts and pursue the debate on a scientific level.

As Matsushige points out, however, scientific validity may not always be a decisive factor in the judgements that patients and their parents make. When patients face medical treatment, scientific evidence is just one of many factors to consider. For example, they must also decide whether their lifestyle can accommodate the cost and length of the treatment, whether it is worth enduring the treatment's side effects, and whether they trust science more than natural treatments in the first place.

Indeed, considering that the potential factors patients may need to consider are too numerous to list, it is clear that the question of whether something is scientifically valid can never necessarily be the only factor patients and their families consider when making judgements. Despite this reality, scientific validity still often goes unchallenged as the sole judgement criterion for the formation of new medical knowledge.

Epstein's example of AIDS activism can certainly be interpreted as a success story of the influence of patient knowledge through scientific engagement. However, this book presents factors other than scientific validity, such as lifestyle and experience, to suggest another dimension of knowledge beyond narrow scientific debates. This book also considers the ways in which these other factors can gain significance.

### What is patient knowledge?

The patient knowledge in the political and scientific debates described earlier counted only insofar as it was scientifically valid, and this raises the question of what *patient knowledge* actually means. In Jeannette Pols's (2014: 75) description, it is '"messy" knowledge, involving many different techniques, values, and materials.' Some aspects of this messy patient knowledge may be scientifically significant, but some may not. For example, Pols describes a case of patients with severe lung disease. These patients struggle with shortness of breath and find it difficult to move around much at all. One patient advised another not to towel themselves off after a shower, but just to put on a bathrobe and passively wait for it to dry them, reasoning that the former requires too much energy and would tire them. While this technique of conserving energy by using a bathrobe has no relation to scientific knowledge, it could certainly be useful and practical advice for patients trying to live their everyday lives. Pols suggests that patient knowledge also includes such non-scientific aspects; in fact, whether the knowledge is scientifically valid or not is simply not important for patients at the practical level.

Patient knowledge is also characterized by individual experiences which cannot always be generalized or applied to other patients. While scientific knowledge is oriented towards generalization, each patient is unique in terms of their body and thoughts. Because of this, the most important concern for patients is not whether the treatment has scientific validity or not, but whether the treatment is effective or suitable for them or not. In this sense, patient knowledge importantly involves the ability to choose the most suitable treatment for the individual. As described later, some patients with severe eczema symptoms found that standard treatment was ineffective at controlling their symptoms. Even if standard treatment works for most patients, this does not mean that other patients' experiences and knowledge should be ignored.

It is, therefore, important to think through what kinds of knowledge should be counted as valid and legitimate. In the medical and scientific realm, scientific evidence is the one that is most validated, especially evidence derived from systematic reviews of research papers involving randomized controlled trials. Clinical trials carefully control for conditions, and the participants are also carefully selected for the purpose of obtaining the purest clinical results. In other words, the most legitimate scientific evidence is derived from strictly controlled situations that are carefully detached from actual living conditions, which inevitably include many variables. However, when these findings are applied to individual patients in the real world, standard treatments or drugs are used in diverse situations by different types of patients. In these contexts, it is always possible that new effects of treatments or drugs will be discovered. In this sense, patients' actual experiences are a source of knowledge which has the potential to challenge the scientific evidence, which is derived only from clinical trials with limited variables.

Thus, even though the scientific evidence produced under strictly controlled situations is highly valued from a scientific point of view, if it is not applicable to the actual lives of patients, it is not meaningful to patients. What types of knowledge, then, should have validity? More fundamentally, how, from which point of view, and for whom should this validity be decided?

## What is atopic dermatitis?

### Defining atopic dermatitis

A precise and concise definition of *atopic dermatitis* is elusive. As discussed later, it is not necessarily a single disease, but rather a collection of varying symptoms with differing causes. Broadly speaking, varying forms of dermatitis from various causes are lumped into the single category of *atopic dermatitis*, which thus cannot be defined as a disease with a specific set of symptoms. The difficulty of defining the disease is apparent in the way in which the standardized name *atopic dermatitis* became established. There were previously a number of different names for the disease, and it is difficult to determine exactly when these symptoms started to appear in the history of human beings.

The first documented evidence of atopic dermatitis is believed to come from Roman historian Suetonius in the 2nd century. He describes the condition of Roman Emperor Augustus's skin as follows:

> He had besides several callosities resembling scars, occasioned by an itching in his body, and the constant and violent use of the strigil in being rubbed.
> (Suetonius, 2017; 100)

Suetonius (2017; 100) also describes the Emperor's tendency to illness:

> He was likewise subject to fits of sickness at stated times every year; for about his birth-day he was commonly a little indisposed. In the beginning of spring, he was attacked with an inflation of the midriff; and when the wind was southerly, with a cold in his head.

Since Augustus' grandson suffered from rhinoconjunctivitis, and another relative had an allergy to horse dander, it is believed that his symptoms were a manifestation of atopic dermatitis (Suetonius, 2017).

In the time between Augustus' reign and the modern era, there was little documented evidence of atopic dermatitis. At the end of the 19th century, however, the notion that nervous system abnormalities, including psychological symptoms, could cause atopic dermatitis surfaced, and the concept of neurodermatitis began to gain popularity. The term *atopy* was first coined in 1923, when Arthur Coca and Robert Cooke defined it as having frequent reactions to environmental allergens and a predisposition to conditions such as eczema, hives, and hay fever. The word *atopy* derives from the ancient Greek *atopia*, meaning 'unusualness, strangeness.' A decade later, in 1933, atopic dermatitis was given its official name, when American dermatologist Dr. Marion B. Sulzberger proposed the name to describe a form of chronic eczema thought to be a constitutional disease of unknown etiology. However, in Northern Europe, at least 12 other names were used in addition to atopic dermatitis until the late 1970s,[4] so the history of atopic dermatitis being recognized as a single disease is remarkably short. The name *atopic dermatitis* was not used in Japan until after the Second World War, as various other terms describing the symptoms had been used instead.

The reason it took so long to establish a universal name is, as discussed previously, the fact that atopic dermatitis is not a disease caused by something as easily identifiable as a pathogen. Atopic dermatitis is a syndrome encompassing a range of symptoms that are a reaction to various internal and external factors, and the potential causes are numerous and diverse. In this sense, the fundamental model of disease causation, in which an external agent brings about disease within a host, fails to apply to atopic dermatitis. Moreover, the disease differs by the individual to such an extent that each patient could be seen as suffering from their own unique disease.

As can be inferred from the aforementioned characteristics, atopic dermatitis is extremely difficult to define. Jon Hanifin and Georg Rajka formed the diagnostic criteria for atopic dermatitis in the 1970s and 1980s, but the criteria they proposed were very difficult to interpret. In order to make a diagnosis of atopic dermatitis, at least three of the following criteria had to be met: (1) pruritus (itching), (2) typical morphology and distribution, (3) chronic or chronically relapsing dermatitis, and (4) a personal or family history of atopy (asthma, allergic rhinitis, or atopic dermatitis). Furthermore, three or more of an additional 23 minor criteria had to be met, and these included xerosis, ichthyosis, immediate (type I) skin test reactivity, elevated serum immunoglobulin E (IgE), and an early age of onset (Williams, 2000).[5] Schultz-Larsen and Hanifin (1992) later developed a questionnaire for the diagnosis of atopic dermatitis with a points-based system that put patients into three, rather than two, categories: having atopic dermatitis, potentially having atopic dermatitis, and not having atopic dermatitis. As we will see, atopic dermatitis is not a choice between two extremes; instead, perhaps better suited to the nature of the disease would be a continuous assessment of the extent of the patient's symptoms.

As such, defining atopic dermatitis is challenging, and slight variations in definitions exist between different countries. In the UK, a somewhat simplified version of Hanifin and Rajka's diagnostic criteria is used for children over four. Firstly, the patient's pruritus must have continued for over 12 months, and then three of the following five criteria must be met: (1) onset under the age of two, (2) history of a flexural involvement, (3) history of a generally dry skin in the last year, (4) personal history of atopic disease, and (5) visible flexural dermatitis (Williams et al., 1994).

In Japan, on the other hand, the definition of atopic dermatitis is as follows:

> Atopic dermatitis is a disease characterized by repeated exacerbations and remissions, in which the chief symptom is itchy lesions, and a large number of patients also display a predisposition to atopy.

Further, a predisposition to atopy is defined by the following two criteria: (1) a family or personal history of one or more of asthma, allergic rhinitis or conjunctivitis, or atopic dermatitis, or (2) a predisposition to produce elevated levels of IgE antibodies (Furue et al., 2009). Although guidelines in both the UK and Japan reference Hanifin and Rajka's diagnostic criteria, the guidelines in each country are simplified versions of them in subtly different ways.

### The number of atopic dermatitis patients in the world

The total number of atopic dermatitis patients in Japan is estimated to be around 456,000. This would mean that around 0.35% of the population is seeking treatment for the disease (Ministry of Health, Labour and Welfare, 2014). It is difficult to find an equivalent total current estimate for the UK, but it has been estimated that 20% of the country could suffer from atopic dermatitis in their lifetime (Kay et al., 1994). The research of Hywel Williams et al. (1999) on global incidence rates is instructive for better comparing the incidence rate of atopic dermatitis in the two countries. Williams's team compared the incidence rates of atopic dermatitis among children aged 6–7 years in 37 countries and children aged 13–14 years in 56 countries (Table 1.1). According to this investigation, the incidence rates among children aged 6–7 years were 16.9% in Japan and 13% in the UK, and those among children aged 13–14 years were 10.5% in Japan and 15.8% in the UK. Incidence rates were thus higher in Japan among children aged 6–7 years, but higher in the UK for children aged 13–14 years.

A study conducted as part of Health and Labour Sciences Research provides an example of a study in Japan regarding rates of prevalence among children. The study was called 'A study into research regarding the number of atopic dermatitis patients and environmental factors that influence the occurrence and exacerbation of the disease,' and it was conducted between 2000 and 2002. It found that the prevalence among first-grade elementary school students in Japan (aged 6–7 years) was 11.8%, and the prevalence among sixth-grade students was 10.6% (Yamamoto and Kawano, 2006). Meanwhile, in the UK, the prevalence among children of school-going age (5–16 years) was found to be between 15% and 20% (Scottish Intercollegiate Guidelines Network, 2011). These results suggest that the prevalence among children is higher in the UK than in Japan.

There are not yet any studies regarding adults on a nationwide scale, but a pilot study conducted as part of Health and Labour Sciences Research between 2003 and 2005 provides some frame of reference. It was titled 'A study into the investigative methodology of atopic dermatitis prevalence rates and how to facilitate a lifestyle environment to prevent and control the disease' and determined the prevalence among 2,123 staff members at Tokyo University. The participants' average age was 38.8 ± 10.4 years, and the overall rate of prevalence was 6.9% (Yamamoto and Kawano, 2006). It has been calculated that between 2% and 10% of British adults have experienced symptoms of atopic dermatitis at some point (Scottish Intercollegiate Guidelines Network, 2011). The overall rate

*Table 1.1* Incidence rates of atopic dermatitis around the world

| Countries | 6–7 years old (%) | 13–14 years old (%) |
| --- | --- | --- |
| Nigeria | – | 17.7 |
| Finland | – | 15.6 |
| Sweden | 18.4 | 14.5 |
| UK | 13 | 15.5 |
| New Zealand | 14.7 | 12.7 |
| Ethiopia | – | 11.4 |
| Japan | 16.9 | 10.8 |
| France | 8.8 | 10 |
| Australia | 10.9 | 9.7 |
| USA | – | 8.5 |
| Thailand | 11.9 | 8.2 |
| Brazil | 7.3 | 5.3 |
| Korea | 8.8 | 3.8 |
| India | 2.7 | 3.8 |
| Iran | 1.1 | 2.6 |
| China | – | 1.2 |

Adapted from Williams et al. (1999).

of adult patients has not been comprehensively calculated in either the UK or Japan, and it is difficult to make comparisons, but these results suggest that the rates of prevalence are similar.

It is believed that rates of atopic dermatitis are rising among developed countries (Ueda, 1998), and relatively high rates have been observed among children aged 13–14 years in European countries, including Sweden (14.5%), Finland (15.6%), and the UK (15.8%), as well as in Oceanian countries, including New Zealand (12.7%) and Australia (9.7%). The incidence rate in Japan (10.5%) is just as high as in these countries, and is the highest recorded rate in Asia. In this investigation, however, African countries, such as Nigeria (17.7%) and Ethiopia (11.4%), showed exceptionally high rates of incidence, suggesting that the theory that rates are higher in developed countries may not necessarily hold true. In any case, since, as already discussed, defining atopic dermatitis is very challenging, it is possible that incidence rates among countries vary depending on the definition used. As a result, one must carefully consider how accurate the comparisons of incidence rates in this study are.

### Atopic dermatitis in Japan

The amount of attention given to atopic dermatitis in Japan might be high compared to other countries, but this seems unrelated to the number of patients suffering from the disease. As previously discussed, it is true that reported incidence rates of atopic dermatitis in Japan are relatively high, but there is little to distinguish them from those of the UK. The term *atopic dermatitis* is considered a medical term in the UK, and is not typically understood by the average person. While the term *eczema*, on the other hand, is widely known, it still does not receive a significant amount of attention in people's daily lives. With the situation in the UK as a point of reference, it seems significant that the term *atopic dermatitis* has gained such widespread recognition in Japan.

The level of awareness of atopic dermatitis in Japan also stands out when compared to that of the USA. In 1997, *The New York Times* ran a story about the atopic dermatitis situation in Japan called 'An Itch Torments Many Japanese, But Relief Is Elusive':

> Atopic dermatitis occurs in the United States as well, but it receives little attention. 'It's kind of a silent epidemic here,' said Dr. Jon M. Hanifin, a professor of dermatology at the Oregon Health Sciences University in Portland, one of the leading American experts.
>
> (Pollack, 1997)

Perhaps the way atopic dermatitis is interpreted in the UK is similar to this situation in the USA. Although there are significant incidence rates, it has mostly escaped recognition. In contrast, atopic dermatitis attracts a reasonable amount of attention in Japan, and there are a significant number of opportunities to hear the term used. A large number of general-audience books regarding the disease have been published, and it is not uncommon to see advertisements in magazines and newspapers promoting treatment or food products aimed at atopic dermatitis patients. There is also an abundance of information regarding the disease on Japanese websites.

Comparing the number of articles in representative newspapers in Japan and the UK helps to illustrate how much more attention atopic dermatitis has received in Japan. Figure 1.1 presents the number of articles in the *Asahi Shimbun*, one of the five national newspapers in Japan, printed each year from 1980 to 2014, on the topic of atopy.[6] It shows how the number of articles relating to atopic dermatitis increased significantly from 1980, reached its peak in 1999,

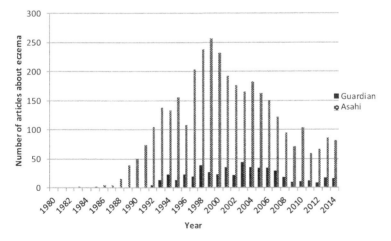

*Figure 1.1* The number of newspaper articles relating to atopy and eczema.

and then started a gradual decline. For a point of reference, the number of articles found in the British newspaper *The Guardian* is also shown. As mentioned previously, since the term *atopic dermatitis* is not widely used in the UK, the more common term *eczema* was used in its place. Although there were some articles on eczema from the 1990s onward in the UK, even at their peak, there were fewer than 50 articles in a year, and there are few fluctuations. When compared to the UK, the number of Japanese articles on atopic dermatitis stands out.

Why has atopic dermatitis been talked about so much in Japan, but not in Western countries such as the UK and the USA? Part of the reason can be found in the so-called steroid bashing of the 1990s and in the associated alternative medicine treatments targeting atopic dermatitis patients, which started to increase around the same time. Dermatologist Kazuhiko Takehara (2000: 8) suggests that confusion surrounding atopic dermatitis is unique to Japan, and the source of this confusion is the existence of what he calls the Atopy Business:

> Medical care for atopic dermatitis is in a state of confusion. What was once seen as a trivial case of dermatitis by qualified dermatologists gained a reputation as an incurable disease before they knew it. When a number of alternative medicine groups, or rather businesses under the guise of alternative medicine, influenced sections of the media to produce misleading reports, an ordinary chronic disease was transformed into a mysterious and incurable one. Dermatology treatment was caught up in the midst of this phenomenon, which was something not seen anywhere else in the world, or indeed anywhere else among skin diseases or allergies other than atopic dermatitis.

For the treatment of other conditions that required steroids, such as psoriasis and asthma, there were no outward signs of a 'Psoriasis Business' or an 'Asthma Business,' so the fact that the Atopy Business appeared for atopic dermatitis is of particular interest. Takehara (2000) indicates a large number of factors that may have contributed to the success of the Atopy Business, including the ambiguity of the name, the lack of a standardized treatment, the large number of patients, the media support for the condition, the fact that it was not a life-threatening disease, and the ability of practitioners to take credit for cures that occurred naturally.

It could also be said that what allowed the majority of these alternative medicine treatments to gain clients was their critical stance on steroids, which are at the core of standard atopic dermatitis treatment. Although steroids are an extremely effective medication that can relieve inflammation almost immediately, their long-term use can lead to various side effects, including atrophy of the skin, hair growth, dilatation of the capillaries, a propensity to bacterial and fungal infections, and blotchy skin. Furthermore, when steroids are discontinued suddenly, many patients can experience a severe exacerbation of symptoms known as a relapse, and their long-term use makes getting off medication increasingly difficult. Topical steroids were first approved in Japan in 1954, and now that several decades have passed, the side effects of steroids have gradually started to become known. The first signs of people beginning to find the limits of steroids and experience frustrations with them seemed to appear between the 1980s and 1990s. This was when alternative medicine treatments first started finding success in capitalizing on patients' desires to avoid using steroids, and the subsequent advertising campaigns and newspaper articles may have been instrumental in atopic dermatitis gaining widespread recognition.

### *The discourse surrounding atopic dermatitis*

This section draws upon magazine articles and other media sources to interrogate how atopic dermatitis has been discussed in different ways at different times. The discourse around steroids and atopic dermatitis from the 1980s until the present day can be split roughly into three stages. The first stage is the so-called steroid bashing that began in the 1980s. The trigger for this criticism was the case of the atopic dermatitis patient Hiroko Ezaki, who filed a suit for damages against her doctor after experiencing side effects from repeated steroid use. The trial continued until 1988 and resulted in the doctor paying ¥5,000,000 (around £35,000 or $45,000) in damages. Ezaki later published a book titled *Kao Tsuburete mo Kagayaite* (*Keep Shining Even If Your Face Is Ruined*), detailing her experience of the trial. The book was a scathing criticism of steroid treatment and the doctors who provide it (Ezaki, 1998).

In the 1990s, warnings regarding steroids began appearing in the media. One of the most notable examples among them was a special report on steroids on the news programme 'News Station' in 1992 titled *Mahō no Kusuri: Steroid-zai no Otoshiana* (*Magic Medicine: The Pitfalls of Steroids*). This programme explained the side effects of topical steroids and the mechanisms behind them, detailing a number of them, including loss of eyesight due to cataracts, decreased resistance to infectious diseases such as herpes, unsightly physical symptoms such as seeping bodily fluids after their long-term use, and mental instability. Later in the programme, the television presenter explained how the patients introduced on the show ultimately gained relief from their symptoms by discontinuing their use of topical steroids. He used these examples to conclude that patients could become dependent on steroids and advised viewers against using them indefinitely (News Station, 1992). A large number of atopic dermatitis patients subsequently developed a fear of steroids, and patients in Japan began to stop using them, a trend that became known as steroid withdrawal treatment. Magazine articles at the time also warned against steroids, as can be seen in the article titles below.

Definitive Edition – New Treatment Guide – Curing Atopic Dermatitis Vol. 3: The Double-Edged Sword of Steroid Medication (*Shūkan Asahi*, 21 June 1991)

Expert Clinic Visitation Diary Vol. 23 – Atopy Clinic – Don't Use Steroids to Extremes, Eliminate the Root Cause for a Cure (*Katei Gahō*, December 1993)
The Forefront of Mind-Body Health – Beating Atopic Dermatitis Part 3: Freeing Yourself from Steroids (*Hanako*, 22 June 1995)

Following on from steroid bashing, the second stage was characterized by a boom in alternative medicine treatments claiming to provide treatment for atopic dermatitis. As the fear of steroids and awareness of their side effects began to spread, there was an explosion in the number of alternative medicine treatments that did not require steroids. A wide range of remedies and treatments began appearing. These ranged from products such as acidic water, soaps, shampoos, atopic vacuum cleaners, futons, creams, and cosmetics, to therapies such as hot spring therapy and hydrotherapy. The majority of the articles related to atopic dermatitis in the 1990s were actually advertisements for alternative medicine treatments. Some examples of articles on alternative medicine are listed below.

Following 'Garlic Baths Healed My Atopy' – Bathing Therapy Using Garlic B1 Extract Bathing Agent (*Shūkan Post*, 23 November 1990)
Miraculous!? My Atopy Is Cured! Kiss Itchiness Goodbye! Life without Steroids – The Top 3 Treatments: Hot Springs, Vaccines, Shampoo (*Shūkan Josei*, 15 December 1992)
Japanese Basil Extract Made My Itchy, Dry Atopic Skin Beautiful Again! (*Bishō*, 7 August 1993)

However, many of these products and treatments were of dubious quality, were incredibly expensive, or, in fact, did make use of steroids. They were part of what doctors using standard treatment referred to as the Atopy Business, and they soon came to be seen as problematic. By the late 1990s, articles such as the following were warning against the Atopy Business.

News Cooking – Illustrated News Commentary – Beware Scammers Exploiting Atopy Patients: How They Pose as Waterworks Employees and Use Futon Cleaning as a Pretext to Hawk Wares (*Shūkan Josei*, 11 November 1997)
Atopic Dermatitis – The Misunderstanding around Steroid Treatment and the Victims of Alternative Therapies It Creates – Plus, the Increasing Sophistication of the Atopy Business (*Science*, 2 October 1998)
Physicians Beware! The Atopy Business Capitalizing on Steroid Phobia – Victims of the Scammers Sowing the Seeds of Fear of Atopy Treatment and Steroids for Profit (*Sunday Mainichi*, 21 March 1999)

In addition to criticism of alternative therapies, articles reversed their position on steroids and came to their defence.

Exhaustive Investigation – Are Steroids Really Evil? The Noise around the Side Effects and Symptoms of Atopy Medication Allowing Scammers to Cash In – We Analyse the Constituents and Efficacy (*Sunday Mainichi*, 4 April 1999)

Atopic Dermatitis – The Increasing Victims of Bogus Treatment: How the Dermatological Association Is Tackling the Problem – Plus, Special Treatment
and Steroid Withdrawal: The Surprising Bogus Treatment in Health Care
(*Saiasu*, June 1999)

The Courage to Speak: 'The Atopy Business Has Little Validity,' Says the Dermatological Association's Investigative Body – An Investigation into the
Harm Caused by Bogus Atopic Dermatitis Treatments (*Shūkan Bunshun*,
22 June 2000)

As the second and third articles show, the turn toward supporting steroids has
a lot to do with support for the Japanese Dermatological Association, an association of Japanese dermatologists which promotes standard steroid treatment.

One important highlight of the third stage was the establishment of a set of
guidelines for atopic dermatitis treatment. Steroid bashing, in addition to the
reality of large numbers of patients refusing steroids at clinics and hospitals at
the time, became a trigger for the formation of these guidelines. In 1999, a research team from the Ministry of Health, Labour and Welfare released guidelines that clearly stated the necessity of steroids for relieving inflammation. Then
in 2000, the Japanese Association of Dermatologists released guidelines that
listed steroids as the first choice for atopic dermatitis treatment. The aim of these
guidelines was to help convince patients who were refusing steroids against their
doctor's advice to start using them, as well as to put a stop to the Atopy Business.
They appeared to succeed in this aim to some extent, as from the 2000s onward,
patients rarely openly refused steroids. With these guidelines established, it is
also fair to say that the once raging tides of steroid bashing abated. The number
of articles on atopic dermatitis decreased in the 2000s, and their tone became
more neutral.[7]

A Crossroads of Health – Let's Cure Adult Atopic Dermatitis and Get Back into
Fashion – The Effect of Protopic Ointment, the Benefits and Side Effects of
Steroids, and More (*Kurashi no Techō*, April 2007)

Junichi Watanabe Gets Up Close with Doctors and Patients – The Latest in
Medicine Vol. 87: Atopic Dermatitis Edition – Atopic Dermatitis Steroid
Medication: To Use or Not to Use? (*Shūkan Gendai*, 31 May 2008)

When the discourse around atopic dermatitis is followed in this way, it is clear
that the debate around steroids is at the centre of it all. It started with steroid
bashing, then there was a boom in alternative medicine treatments, and finally
there was the subsequent criticism of those treatments and renewed support for
steroids. Furthermore, when viewing the situation this way, it is evident that
only steroids have received this attention, making it seem as if only steroids are
used to treat atopic dermatitis; however, both tacrolimus ointment (Protopic
ointment) and ciclosporin (Neoral) are also used in modern treatment. Tacrolimus ointment was first used in Japan, ahead of other countries, in 1999, and
within four years, it had come to be used to treat atopic dermatitis in ten more
countries around the world. Tacrolimus is an immunosuppressive drug, which

was originally used to suppress the rejection response in patients undergoing organ transplants, but it later came to be used for atopic dermatitis treatment. It is generally applied to the face, where large amounts of steroids cannot be used, and often acts as a substitute for steroids. However, a study found that applying tacrolimus to the bodies of mice increased the incidence of cancer, which has raised some concerns regarding its safety.

Ciclosporin is also an immunosuppressive drug used, for example, to suppress the rejection response in organ transplant patients and to treat autoimmune disease. In 2008, it was approved for use in the treatment of atopic dermatitis, and it has since been used for severe cases in which steroids fail to have any effect. The side effects include impairment of kidney function, hypertension, hair growth, and enlargement of the gums.

Medication other than steroids is now used in the treatment of atopic dermatitis, but tacrolimus ointment and ciclosporin have not yet received the kind of criticism that has been directed at steroids. This is perhaps due to the general lack of awareness of them on account of their short history as atopic dermatitis treatments and the fact that they only act as a substitute for steroids, the first-choice treatment. In contrast, as atopic dermatitis has entered the public awareness, there has been strong interest and debate surrounding steroids. Indeed, if it were not for the problems surrounding steroids, perhaps atopic dermatitis would not have gained the recognition it has.

## Research methods and chapter outline

### *The research methods*

This research is based on anthropological fieldwork. Unlike most social scientific approaches, anthropological research aims not to find data that can be generalized, but to find data that are often highly particular and difficult to generalize. Because of this, many anthropologists conduct participant observation and find their informants using the snowball sampling technique, and my methods were no exception. I conducted participant observation at two self-help groups in Japan for seven years and at one self-help group in the UK for four years. I built up a rapport with the patients I met there and found informants through the snowball sampling technique.

I conducted interviews in Japan between 2005 and 2013 with sixteen female patients, twelve male patients, and four male doctors. Among the twenty-eight patients, at the time of the interview, thirteen were undergoing standard steroid treatment, eight had discontinued steroids, and the remaining seven had experienced steroid withdrawal in the past but had resumed treatment. Among the four doctors, two were dermatologists, one had changed his specialty from dermatology to plastic surgery, and one was a paediatrician.

I came to know 11 of the patients through meetings or camps organized by an authorized NPO called Atopicco Network for Children of the Earth. I met seven of them through Atopy-free.com, and the remaining ten were already acquaintances of mine or were introduced through acquaintances as atopic dermatitis patients. Of the doctors, I came to know three of them through meetings organized by Atopicco Network for Children of the Earth, and one of these doctors introduced me to the other one.

Thus, I met around two-thirds of the interview participants for this investigation through Atopicco Network for Children of the Earth and Atopy-free.com, as self-help groups such as these tend to have a higher concentration of patients with severe symptoms and patients who have attempted to discontinue standard steroid treatment. Since this investigation centred on this type of patient, it should be noted that there may be some bias in the sample.

Excluding my time spent back in Japan, I resided a total of two years and nine months in the UK between 2008 and 2012, and I conducted interviews in the UK between 2008 and 2011. Interview participants comprised seven female patients, seven male patients, and one male practitioner of alternative medicine. Seven of the patients were British, two Japanese, one Australian, one Polish, one Filipino, one Bangladeshi, and one of unknown nationality. This range of nationalities is thanks to the ethnic diversity of London, where the interviews were carried out. I met four of these British patients through the National Eczema Society (NES), two Japanese and two British patients were introduced to me through acquaintances, and I found the remaining patients through the classifieds website Gumtree. I posted a classified ad for volunteers on Gumtree and interviewed the respondents. Of those interviewed through Gumtree, five turned out to be foreign residents in the UK, and one was a British citizen. I was introduced to the practitioner of alternative medicine by an acquaintance.

The interviews in both Japanese and English were based on 13 prepared questions. As semi-structured interviews, I elicited further expansion from participants while asking these questions. The majority of the questions focused on understanding the participant's life story, and I dedicated the most time to this investigation. The interview location was chosen at the participant's convenience (e.g., a cafe, a university classroom, or their home), and efforts were made to create an environment in which the participants felt comfortable speaking freely. Participants signed an interview consent form prior to their interview, and interviews were recorded when recording permission was obtained. Only one participant declined to allow recording, and consent to record was obtained in all other cases. Interviews lasted between one hour to one and a half hours, and the recordings were transcribed afterwards. Interviews were conducted between one to four times for each participant, and those who consented to multiple interviews were interviewed over a number of years. All names, except for one Japanese doctor who gave me permission to use his real name, have been changed in this book to protect the privacy of the participants.

## Chapter outline

This book is composed of six chapters. In Chapter 1, I summarize the research regarding the doctor–patient relationship and patient knowledge, and I show

how patient stories have gained increasing attention as cases of chronic diseases have increased. This chapter goes on to explain how this trend has led to an increasing recognition of patient knowledge alongside the professional knowledge of doctors.

The next four chapters (Chapters 2–5) detail where patients go to seek treatment. When patients fall ill, they visit not only clinics or hospitals, but also alternative medicine practitioners and self-help groups. Chapter 2 outlines and introduces the various sectors that influence patients in both Japan and the UK. These sectors fall into three categories: the professional sector, the folk sector, and the popular sector. Chapter 3 focuses on the professional sector, which includes modern medical treatment as well as steroid withdrawal doctors who provide treatment without the use of topical steroids. Since the media commotion in Japan about the side effects of topical steroids in the 1990s, the number of patients wishing to discontinue topical steroids has increased, and steroid withdrawal doctors have appeared to offer support. This chapter compares the professional sectors in Japan and the UK. The most important difference between them is that there are conflicting opinions about steroids among doctors in Japan, but not in the UK. I investigate the explanatory models in Japan for standard treatment and steroid withdrawal treatment, and I illustrate how these conflict. On the other hand, in the UK, there is no conflict among doctors because no doctors provide steroid withdrawal treatment. The professional sector in the UK only provides treatment which is basically the same as the standard treatment in Japan.

Chapter 4 then introduces alternative medicine as it is practised in Japan and the UK. *Alternative medicine* refers to all medical treatments not part of modern medicine, and this includes anything from traditional Chinese medicine to homeopathy and hot spring therapy. Despite this diversity, it is possible to find common characteristics among these therapies, such as a general impression of a lack of harmful side effects and the promise of hope. There are a greater number of these therapies in Japan, and they form a hodgepodge of uneven quality, whereas the industry in Britain has reached a relatively well-regulated state.

In Chapter 5, I introduce in the context of Japan, the self-help group Atopy-free.com and Atopicco Network for Children of the Earth, and in the UK, the self-help group National Eczema Society. Although all are broadly referred to as self-help groups, the activities and aims of each group differ.

Chapter 6 then considers scientific evidence and patient knowledge in light of the patient case studies presented in the previous chapters. The problem here is that scientific evidence drawn from statistics does not necessarily apply to patients on a case-by-case basis. Even when undergoing a treatment with 90% efficacy, patients may find themselves falling into the remaining 10%. Patients are interested in the highly personal problem of how it all applies to them specifically. As a result, statistical scientific evidence and the opinions of patients can end up at odds with each other. In carrying out treatment that respects patient knowledge, it is important to consider the extent to which the patient's thoughts should influence the selection of treatment.

There are aspects of patient knowledge which aim to revolutionize medical science, but there is also what could be called local or living knowledge, which has no relationship to the grand debates of medical science. Doctors and scientists value scientific knowledge that could revolutionize medicine, but many patients have a stronger interest in knowledge more closely related to their daily lives, such as how to balance their symptoms with their job or what kind of food is good for them. As a result, it is necessary to recognize that the scientific knowledge at the centre of medical treatment is not the only knowledge with value.

## Notes

1 'Atopic dermatitis' and 'eczema' indicate same symptoms. However, 'atopic dermatitis' is commonly used in Japan, and 'eczema' in the UK. Thus, this book uses the former to refer to the situation in Japan and the latter for the UK. For medical explanations, this book uses the term 'atopic dermatitis' as this is the official medical term.

2 The steroids used for inflammation of the skin are glucocorticoids and are in a different class to the anabolic steroids used to promote muscle growth that appear in doping scandals.

3 In order for a drug to be approved, it must meet the criteria defined by the Ministry of Health, Labour and Welfare, and clinical trials are scientific studies carried out to attain approval. If an adequate level of efficacy and safety cannot be confirmed through clinical trials, then the drug will not be approved.

4 The 12 names are eczema, atopic eczema, infantile eczema, eczéma constitutionnel, flexural eczema, prurigo Besnier, allergic eczema, childhood eczema, Lichen Vidal, endogenous eczema, spätexsudatives Ekzematoid, and neurodermatitis (Williams, 2000).

5 The 23 minor symptoms are as follows: (1) xerosis, (2) ichthyosis/palmar hyperlinearity, keratosis pilaris, (3) immediate (type I) skin test reaction, (4) elevated serum IgE, (5) early age of onset, (6) tendency towards cutaneous infections (especially *Staphylococcus. aureus* and herpes simplex), impaired cell-mediated immunity, (7) tendency towards non-specific hand or foot dermatitis, (8) nipple eczema, (9) cheilitis, (10) recurrent conjunctivitis, (11) Dennie–Morgan infraorbital fold, (12) keratoconus, (13) anterior subcapsular cataracts, (14) orbital darkening, (15) facial pallor, facial erythema, (16) pityriasis alba, (17) anterior neck folds, (18) itch when sweating, (19) intolerance to wool and lipid solvents, (20) periofollicular accentuation, (21) food intolerance, (22) course influenced by environmental and emotional factors, and (23) white dermographism, delayed blanch (Williams, 2000).

6 In Japan, the term 'atopy' is commonly used in lieu of 'atopic dermatitis,' and this is the reason why this term is used while searching the articles.

7 However, various self-help groups and steroid withdrawal doctors argue that the establishment of the standard treatment guidelines made the situation worse. By using steroids, the number of patients who are able to control their symptoms and improve their quality of life may have increased. However, the long-term use of steroids itself is a problem because it is also likely that the number of patients who see no improvement in their atopic dermatitis and the diminishing effectiveness of steroids will also increase (Fukaya, 2010).

# References

Arksey, H. 1998, *RSI and the experts: the construction of medical knowledge*, London: UCL Press.

Brown, P. 2007, *Toxic exposures: contested illnesses and the environmental health movement*, New York: Columbia University Press.

Brown, P., Morello-Frosch R. & Zavestoski, S. 2011, *Contested illnesses: citizens, science, and health social movements*, Berkeley: University of California Press.

Callon, M. & Rabeharisoa, V. 2003, "Research "in the wild" and the shaping of new social identities", *Technology in Society*, vol. 25, no. 2, pp. 193–204.

Crossley, N. 2006, *Contesting psychiatry: social movements in mental health*, London: Routledge.

Department of Health. 2001, *The expert patient: a new approach to chronic disease management for the 21st century*, London: Crown Copyright.

Epstein, S. 1996, *Impure science: AIDS, activism, and the politics of knowledge*, Berkeley: University of California Press.

Ezaki, H. 1988, *Kao Tsuburetemo Kagayaite: Steroid Nankōka Soshō 6-nen no Kiroku* (*Keep shining even if your face is ruined: six years of steroid ointment litigation*), Tokyo: Ikkōsha.

Freidson, E. 1970, *Professional dominance: the social structure of medical care*, 1st ed., New Brunswick: Aldine; Atherton Press.

Fukaya, M. 2010, *Steroid Izon 2010: Nihon Hifukagakkai wa Atopīseihifuen Shinryō Guideline wo Syūsei Seyo* (*Steroid Addiction 2010: Alter the Guideline of Atopic Dermatitis by Japanese Dermatological Association*), Tokyo: Iyaku Bijiransu Center.

Furue, M., Saeki, H., Furukawa, F., Hide, M., Ohtsuki, M., Katayama, I., Sasaki, R., Sudō, H. & Takehara, K. 2009, "Atopīseihifuen shinryō guideline (Guidelines for Atopic Dermatitis Treatment)", In *Nihon Hifuka Gakkaishi* (*The Japanese Journal of Dermatology*), vol. 119, no. 8, pp. 1515–1534.

Good, B. 1994, *Medicine, rationality, and experience: an anthropological perspective*, Cambridge: Cambridge University Press.

Greenhalgh, T. & Hurwitz, B. 1998, *Narrative based medicine: dialogue and discourse in clinical practice*, London: BMJ.

Hess, D. J. 1999, *Evaluating alternative cancer therapies: a guide to the science and politics of an emerging medical field*, New Brunswick: Rutgers University Press.

Kay, J., Gawkrodger, D. J., Mortimer, M. J. & Jaron, A. G. 1994, "The prevalence of childhood atopic eczema in a general population", *Journal of the American Academy of Dermatology*, vol. 30, no. 1, pp. 35–39.

Klawiter, M. 2008, *The biopolitics of breast cancer: changing cultures of disease and activism*, Minneapolis: University of Minnesota Press.

Kleinman, A. 1988, *The illness narratives: suffering, healing, and the human condition*, New York: Basic Books.

Kodama, Y. 1998, *'Byōki' no Tanjyō: Kindai Iryō no Kigen* (*Birth of 'disease': the origin of modern medicine*), Tokyo: Heibonsha.

Larsen, F. S., & Hanifin, J. M. 1992, "Secular change in the occurrence of atopic dermatitis", *Acta dermato-venereologica. Supplementum*, vol. 176, pp. 7–12.

Latour, B. 1987, *Science in action: how to follow scientists and engineers through society*, Milton Keynes: Open University Press.

Ley, B. L. 2009, *From pink to green: disease prevention and the environmental breast cancer movement*, New Brunswick: Rutgers University Press.

Luger, T. A., Lahfa, M., Fölster-Holst, R., Gulliver, W. P., Allen, R., Molloy, S., Barbier, N., Paul, C. & Bos, J. D. 2004, "Long-term safety and tolerability of pimecrolimus cream 1% and topical corticosteroids in adults with moderate to severe atopic dermatitis", *Journal of Dermatological Treatment*, vol. 15, no. 3, pp. 169–178.

Matsushige, T. 2010, *Kanjya Chūshin no Iryō toiu Gensetsu: Kanjya no 'Chi' no Shakaigaku* (*The theory of 'patient-centered medicine': sociology of patient 'knowledge'*), Tokyo: Rikkyo University Press.

McCormic, S. 2009, *No family history: the environmental links to breast cancer*, Lanham: Rowman & Littlefield publishers.

McKevitt, C. 2013, "Experience, knowledge and evidence: a comparison of research relations in health and anthropology", *Evidence and Policy: A Journal of Research, Debate and Practice, The Policy Press, University of Bristol*, vol. 9, no. 1, pp. 113–130.

Ministry of Health, Labour and Welfare. 2014, "Kanjya chōsa: shippei bunrui hen (Patients survey: sorted by diseases)", viewed 21 March 2019, www.mhlw.go.jp/toukei/saikin/hw/kanja/10syoubyo/index.html.

Murakami, Y. 2002, "Atarashii ishi kanjya kankei (Doctor-patient relations revisited)", *100-syūnen Kinen Symposium* (*100th Anniversary Symposium*), Tokyo: Nihon Igakkai, pp. 6–10.

*News Station*. 1992, Asahi TV.

O'Connor, B. B. 1995, *Healing traditions: alternative medicine and the health professions*, Philadelphia: University of Pennsylvania Press.

O'donovan, O., Moreira, T. & Howlett, E. 2013, "Tracking transformations in health movement organisations: Alzheimer's disease organisations and their changing 'cause regimes", *Social Movement Studies*, vol. 12, no. 3, pp. 316–334.

Panofsky, A. 2011, "Generating sociability to drive science: patient advocacy organizations and genetics research", *Social Studies of Science*, vol. 41, no. 1, pp. 31–57.

Pollack, A. 1997, "An itch torments many Japanese, but relief is elusive", *The New York Times*, August 19. viewed 21 March 2019, www.nytimes.com/1997/08/19/science/an-itch-torments-many-japanese-but-relief-is-elusive.html.

Pols, J. 2014, "Knowing patients: turning patient knowledge into science", *Science, Technology, & Human Values*, vol. 39, no. 1, pp. 73–97.

Porter, R. 1989, *Health for sale: quackery in England, 1660–1850*, Manchester: Manchester University Press.

Scottish Intercollegiate Guidelines Network. 2011, "Management of atopic eczema in primary care: a national clinical guideline", viewed 21 March 2019, www.sign.ac.uk/assets/sign125.pdf.

Suetonius. 2017, *The lives of the twelve Caesars complete*, Available at www.amazon.co.uk/kindlestore (Downloaded: 2 September 2017).

Takehara, K. 2000, *Atopī Business* (*The atopy business*), Tokyo: Bungeishunjyū.

Ueda, H. 1998, "Atopīseihifuen ha zōka shitaka (Has the number of atopic dermatitis patients increased?)" In Yoshida, H. (ed.) *Atopīseihifuen* (*Atopic dermatitis*), Tokyo: Nippon Hyōronsha, pp. 27–38.

Williams, H. C. 2000, "What is atopic dermatitis and how should it be defined in epidemiological studies?" In Williams, H. C. (ed.) *Atopic dermatitis: the epidemiology, causes, and prevention of atopic eczema*, Cambridge: Cambridge University Press, pp. 3–24.

Williams, H. C., Burney, P. G. J., Pembroke, A. C. & Hay, R. 1994, "The U.K. Working Party's Diagnostic Criteria for Atopic Dermatitis. III. Independent hospital validation", *The British Journal of Dermatology*, vol. 131, pp. 406–416.

Williams, H., Robertson, C., Stewart, A., Aït-Khaled, N., Anabwani, G., Anderson, R., Asher, I., Beasley, R., Björkstén, B., Burr, M., Clayton, T., Crane, J., Ellwood, P., Keil, U., Lai, C., Mallol, J., Martinez, F., Mitchell, E., Montefort, S., Pearce, N., Shah, J., Sibbald, B., Strachan, D., von Mutius, E. & Weiland, S. K. 1999, "Worldwide variations in the prevalence of symptoms of atopic eczema in the international study of asthma and allergies in childhood", *Journal of Allergy and Clinical Immunology,* vol. 103, no. 1, pp. 125–138.

Yamamoto, S. & Kawano, Y. 2006, *Atopīseihifuen Shinryō Guideline 2006 (Guidelines for atopic dermatitis treatment 2006)*, Tokyo: Kyōwa Kikaku.

# 2 The sectors surrounding patients

The views of doctors on topical steroids are often at odds with those of patients. Many patients are concerned about the side effects of steroids and would prefer to avoid using them whenever possible. Doctors, on the other hand, are more concerned about patients' symptoms worsening when they stop using their medication and thus try to persuade them to continue their use. Moreover, doctors tend to believe that knowledge gained at medical school or in clinical settings is absolute, but for patients, this professional knowledge is simply one of many perspectives. Patients form their own knowledge as they are exposed to multiple viewpoints, which they then try to apply to their own situations, and this differs from the professional knowledge of doctors.

This chapter aims to demonstrate that multiple places of treatment can exist for a single disease and that each of these places has a different understanding of the disease.

## The three sectors: the professional sector, the folk sector, and the popular sector

When people fall ill, clinics and hospitals are not the only places that can help. Various other options are available to patients beyond the doctor's office, from being taken care of at home by a family member to visiting an alternative medicine practitioner. Medical anthropologist Arthur Kleinman categorized these various places into three sectors: the professional sector, the popular sector, and the folk sector (Figure 2.1). The professional sector essentially refers to modern medicine, but also includes institutionalized forms of traditional medicine, such as traditional Chinese medicine (TCM) in China or Ayurveda in India. The popular sector is the realm of amateurs and includes patients themselves, their family, their social network, and the local community. The folk sector refers to non-professional or non-bureaucratic expert positions; these include bone-setters and herb doctors in Taiwan, shamans, fortune-tellers, astrologists, physiognomists, feng shui masters, medicine sellers, masseurs, breathing exercise instructors, stretching instructors or practitioners, and midwives. However, as Kleinman points out, practitioners in the folk sector have entered into health care in the popular sector, so these two sectors are closely related and difficult to separate clearly.

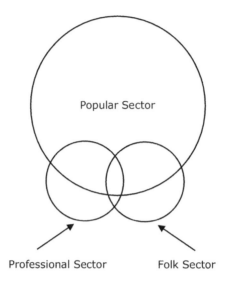

*Figure 2.1* Kleinman's categories (adapted from Kleinman, 1981).

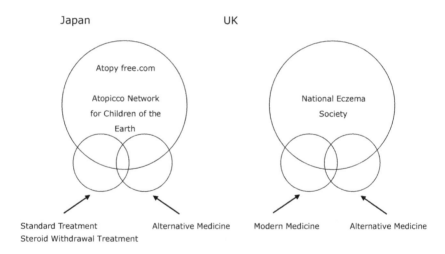

*Figure 2.2* The sectors and groups for atopic dermatitis care.

Building on Kleinman's three-sector framework, this chapter will introduce the multiple sectors that exist in Japan and the UK (Figure 2.2).

The professional sector refers to the legally recognized professional health care sector, which is typified by modern medicine. Standard treatment, as it is known in Japan, matches this definition exactly. Since the term *standard treatment* is not used in the UK, the term *modern medicine* is used instead to refer to this treatment, but they are essentially equivalent.

Doctors who provide treatment without the use of topical steroids would also be placed in the professional sector. Even though the treatment they administer contradicts the theories of modern medicine and has more in common with the steroid withdrawal treatment carried out in the folk sector, they are, as licensed dermatologists, institutionally part of the professional sector.

The so-called folk or alternative medicine falls into the category of the folk sector. Mitsuho Ikeda (1995) defined *alternative medicine* as a leftover category, which includes anything and everything outside of modern medicine, and the folk sector itself could be seen as the true leftover category. Treatments such as hot spring therapy, chlorella, and water therapy, which were ridiculed as being part of the Atopy Business, would certainly be placed into this category.

The popular sector, meanwhile, includes NPOs, NGOs and other self-help groups for patients. This sector is synonymous with those referred to as the *third sector*, and *cooperative sector*, and includes groups or organizations that are neither state-run nor privately run, but rather are formed by members of the public. The groups and organizations introduced in this book fall into this category, and these include Atopy-free.com and Atopicco Network for Children of the Earth in Japan, and the National Eczema Society in the UK.

## Medical pluralism and complementary relationships

It is becoming clearer how the various sectors surrounding atopic dermatitis exist alongside each other, and the following chapters will expand on this understanding with a focus on the relationships between them. Two theories underlie this premise: medical pluralism and complementarity.

The theory of medical pluralism has been promoted by anthropologists such as Charles Miller Leslie and expresses the fact that in many societies, various forms of health care exist in addition to modern medicine, such as Oriental medicine, Ayurveda, or homeopathy. This is an idea that challenges the common association of the term *health care* with modern medicine. Leslie (1976) explains how traditional and alternative medicines have gained some level of legitimacy alongside modern medicine and real acceptance within societies. He points to examples such as China, where TCM exists alongside modern medicine, and India, where Ayurveda, homeopathy, and Unani medicine exist alongside modern medicine. Emiko Ohnuki-Tierney (1984), who conducted research on health care in Japan, also describes how deeply rooted religion, traditional Japanese medicine, and biomedicine are used in treatment within Japanese society.

The greatest achievement of the medical pluralists has been to demonstrate that no matter how strong the influx of modern medicine is, traditional and alternative medicines find a way to continue surviving. This finding belies the general perception that the introduction of superior modern medicine will naturally lead to a decline in inferior forms of health care.

The second theory, complementarity, further explains why traditional and alternative medicines survive. Anthropologist John M. Janzen investigated how the introduction of modern medicine in Zaire affected native forms of health care. He gave the following summary:

> The people of Zaire recognize the advantages of Western medicine and seek its drugs, surgery, and hospital care, but contrary to what might have been expected, native doctors, prophets, and traditional consultations among kinsmen do not disappear with the adoption of Western medicine.
>
> (Janzen, 1978: 3)

Janzen explains that by playing a complementary role to modern medicine, native medicine did not decline, but actually continued to evolve. The view that treatments other than modern medicine can be complementary is a key point in this book. One explanation for the complementary relationship described by Janzen is given by Namihira's question of why, given the level of progress of health care in Japan, there are still people who go to shamans for medical advice. Emiko Namihira (1990) explains how people who visit shamans for medical advice go not only for problems regarding their own illness, which can be treated by the health care system, but for all kinds of personal issues, including those involving their family. Since the needs of these patients cannot necessarily be met by the health care system, shamans and their like are able to fill that void. In this way, modern medicine and other forms of health care are able to form a mutually complementary relationship. The more modern medicine becomes dominant, the more things it leaves unattended, which puts traditional and alternative medicine in a position to pick up the leftover pieces.

This complementary relationship not only applies to cases where modern medicine is introduced alongside native medicine, but can also be seen in cases where alternative medicine prospered after the dominance of modern medicine. In 20th-century Japan and Western Europe, various forms of alternative medicine began to gain success, including Chinese herbal medicine, homeopathy, chiropractic, acupuncture, herbal medicine, and reflexology. The majority of these treatments were suppressed by the overwhelming dominance of modern medicine in the 19th century, but alternative medicine claimed something of a revival as modern medicine continued to evolve throughout the 19th century. If this revival is thought of as having filled the void left by the shortcomings of modern medicine, it could go some way towards explaining the theory of a complementary relationship between them. Examples of modern medicine's shortcomings could be the associated short consultation times, its non-humanistic approach that focuses on diseases rather than on patients, and biochemical side effects. Alternative medicine, conversely often associated with lengthy consultation times, a humanistic approach, and natural remedies free of side effects, could be seen as at the opposite extreme of modern medicine. When looked at in this way, it is easy to see how alternative medicine could appeal to patients as a complement to modern medicine by meeting their unfulfilled needs. Mitsuho Ikeda (1995), Kōichiro Kuroda (2000), Junichi Satō (2000), and Kiyoshi Muraoka (2000) explain how alternative medicine is able to survive by focusing on those patients who have been failed by modern medicine, and by giving them exactly what modern medicine cannot.

Janzen's (1978) research on native health care and Ikeda (1995) and others' research on modern forms of alternative medicine support the idea of alternative medicine as a complement to modern medicine, and this view overlaps with the perspective of this book. This book will examine these ideas further by attempting to explain the kind of complementary relationships that exist among standard treatment, steroid withdrawal doctors, alternative medicine, and self-help groups.

## References

Ikeda, M. 1995, "Hi-seiyō iryō (Non-western medicine)", In Kuroda, K. (ed.) *Gendai Iryō no Shakaigaku (Sociology of modern medicine)*, Kyoto: Sekai Shisōsha, pp. 202–224.

Janzen, J. M. 1978, *The quest for therapy in Lower Zaire*, Berkeley: University of California Press.

Kleinman, A. 1981, *Patients and healers in the context of culture: an exploration of the borderland between anthropology, medicine, and psychiatry*, Berkeley: University of California Press.

Kuroda, K. 2000, "Minkan iryō to seitō iryō no chiseigakuteki 'kankei' (The geopolitical 'relationship' between folk medicine and orthodox medicine)", In Satō, J. (ed.) *Bunka Genshō toshite no Iyashi: Minkan Iryō no Genzai (Healing as a cultural phenomenon: the current status of folk medicine)*, Osaka: Medicus Shuppan, pp. 143–184.

Leslie, C. 1976, "Pluralism and integration in the Indian and Chinese medical systems", In Kleinman, A., Kunstadter, P., Alexander, W. R. & Gale J. S. (eds.) *Medicine in Chinese cultures: comparative studies of health care in Chinese and other societies*, Bethesda: National Institutes of Health, pp. 401–417.

Muraoka, K. 2000, "Minkan iryō no anatomy (Anatomy of folk medicine)", In Satō, J. (ed.) *Bunka Genshō toshite no Iyashi: Minkan Iryō no Genzai (Healing as a cultural phenomenon: the current status of folk medicine)*, Osaka: Medicus Shuppan, pp. 37–76.

Namihira, E. 1990, *Yamai to Shi no Bunka: Gendai Iryō no Jinruigaku (The culture of disease and death: anthropology of modern medicine)*, Tokyo: Asahi Shimbunsha.

Ohnuki-Tierney, E. 1984, *Illness and culture in contemporary Japan: an anthropological view*, Cambridge: Cambridge University Press.

Satō, J. 2000, "Minkan iryō ni asu wa aruka?: minkan iryō no mirai gaku (Can folk medicine survive?: the future of folk medicine)", In Satō. J. (ed.) *Bunka Genshō toshite no Iyashi: Minkan Iryō no Genzai (Healing as a cultural phenomenon: the current status of folk medicine)*, Osaka: Medicus Shuppan, pp. 285–306.

# 3   The professional sector
## Standard treatment and modern medicine

### Standard treatment in Japan

The professional sector generally refers to modern medicine. In Japan and the UK, this is treatment received at a regular clinic or hospital. Since modern medicine is based on science and is not usually influenced by cultural differences between countries, treatment is typically the same around the world. This holds true for atopic dermatitis treatment in Japan and the UK, though there are differences in terminology. Atopic dermatitis treatment based on modern medicine in Japan has come to be referred to as *standard treatment*, a term uncommon in the UK, where treatment is generally referred to simply as *modern medicine*.

The term *standard treatment* came into use around 1990, when guidelines for the treatment of atopic dermatitis were established. The motivation for creating these guidelines was likely the desire of doctors to assert the legitimacy of their treatment over the various treatments and forms of alternative medicine that had appeared in order to wean patients off steroids. However, as there was no such trend toward rebellious treatments in the UK, where the main form of treatment remained modern medicine, it can be assumed that there was little need to explicitly refer to this as *standard treatment*.

### Standard treatment guidelines in Japan

Standard treatment for atopic dermatitis refers to scientifically grounded treatment based on the guidelines set by the Japanese Dermatological Association (Japan Allergy Tomono Kai, 2010). There have thus far been four sets of guidelines for standard treatment for atopic dermatitis in Japan. The first, *Treatment Guidelines for Allergic Diseases*, was based on a special symposium at the fifth spring meeting of the Japanese Society of Allergology in 1993. The second, *Atopic Dermatitis Treatment Guidelines 1999*, was announced by the atopic dermatitis team for the allergy research division of the Ministry of Health and Welfare chronic diseases research initiative. A revised edition of this second set was released in 2005 as *Atopic Dermatitis Treatment Guidelines 2005*. The third set of guidelines, *Atopic Dermatitis Treatment Guidelines 2006*, was based on this revised edition and released by the Japanese Society of Allergology. This set was a more detailed and explanatory version of the relatively simple 2005 revision of the guidelines. In addition, this third set of guidelines was created with multiple branches of medicine in mind, and these guidelines were written by a team of dermatologists and paediatricians, with participation from internal medicine specialists where necessary (Yamamoto and Kawano, 2006).

The fourth set is the *Atopic Dermatitis Treatment Guidelines* created by the Japanese Dermatological Association. These guidelines were originally released in 2000, and revised editions have followed in 2003, 2004, 2008, 2009, and 2016. They have been written specifically for dermatology specialists. The next section presents an outline of these Japanese Dermatological Association guidelines in order to provide a clearer idea of what exactly standard treatment is.

### The goals of treatment

Firstly, the aim of standard treatment is to achieve the following conditions for patients:

> The goal of treatment is to keep the condition symptomless. If symptoms are present, then they should not affect patients' daily life and should require little to no drug therapy. Even if this level is not achieved, the goal is to keep the symptoms slight. Acute exacerbations should be rare and not protracted should they occur.
>
> (Katō et al., 2016: 126)

As discussed in more detail later, standard treatment and steroid withdrawal treatment differ in their goals. Steroid withdrawal treatment can actually induce severe rebounds in having patients discontinue steroid medication. Standard treatment, on the other hand, aims to avoid such exacerbations and to preserve a state as close to symptomless as possible, and drug therapy centred around steroids is at the core of this treatment. The guidelines contain the following description regarding drug therapy:

> Atopic dermatitis is a polygenic disease with causes that include genetic predisposition. There is no drug therapy that can cure the disease, and, as such, it is the standard to provide symptomatic treatment.
>
> (Furue et al., 2009: 1521)

Standard treatment can at most provide symptomatic treatment through the use of drugs. This is in stark contrast to steroid withdrawal treatment, which aims to cure atopic dermatitis itself, or at least alleviate its symptoms, by discontinuing the use of steroids.

## Drug therapy

At the present time in Japan, the only medications that have scientifically demon-strated their efficacy and safety in relieving the inflammation associated with atopic dermatitis are topical steroids and the two immunosuppressive drugs dis-cussed earlier, tacrolimus ointment (Protopic ointment) and ciclosporin (Neo-ral). Oral medications such as oral steroids and ciclosporin (Neoral) are used very rarely and only in extremely severe cases. In most cases, only topical medications such as topical steroids and tacrolimus ointment (Protopic ointment) are applied.

Tacrolimus ointment suppresses inflammation through a mechanism different from topical steroids. It was first sold as an ointment designed for treating atopic dermatitis in 1999 under the name Protopic. Current standard treatment relies primarily on topical steroids supplemented by tacrolimus.

The following is a vastly simplified explanation of how topical steroids and tacrolimus ointment are used. The potency of topical steroids is different for each affected area. This is to avoid using higher strengths than necessary. For example, since the absorption rate of the facial skin is 13 times that of the arm, a suitably weaker steroid is chosen for the face. When symptoms flare up, top-ical steroids are applied twice a day, in which case the potency of the steroids should be gradually decreased or an alternative medication not containing ster-oids should be used. One should then limit the rate of application to once a day or once every other day, while taking care to confirm that there is no reoccur-rence of symptoms. Discontinuing steroids suddenly is certainly something to be avoided.

Side effects are a concern, but are seen as manageable:

> In terms of systemic side effects, some studies report that applying strong topical steroids can suppress adrenal function in some cases, but there will be no suppression of adrenal function or growth failure with milder topical steroids. If topical steroids are applied appropriately, there will be few sys-temic side effects and their safety level is high. In terms of local side effects, atrophy of the skin, capillary dilatation, steroid acne, steroid rosacea, hair growth, stretch marks, and bacterial/fungal/viral skin infections may oc-cur, but discontinuing use and applying other suitable measures will resolve basically everything but stretch marks.
>
> (Katō et al., 2016: 129)

It is thus acknowledged that using strong topical steroids can suppress adrenal function. The adrenal glands release hormones that suppress inflammation. The body naturally produces steroid hormones, but using topical steroids can re-duce this natural production ability. This is what suppressed adrenal function refers to.

Tacrolimus ointment is often used when steroids alone are not sufficient, or when patients display a severe adverse reaction to steroids. This ointment is also often used on sensitive areas such as the face, where the decision to use steroids cannot be taken lightly. As with steroids, the guidelines state that the dosage of tacrolimus ointment should be gradually reduced.

Side effects that include irritative symptoms, such as a burning sensation when applied or hot flashes, can arise when using tacrolimus ointment, though they typically resolve themselves. Since tacrolimus ointment is an immunosuppressive drug, there is also a possibility of contracting skin infections. In addition, patients may experience breakouts of acne and rosacea-like dermatitis. Even more troublingly, incidences of lymphoma and skin cancer have also been reported in studies conducted on mice.

### The problems with standard treatment

Applying topical steroids or tacrolimus ointment until symptoms come under control, as per the guidelines of Japanese Dermatological Association, is likely a very effective treatment for many atopic dermatitis patients. In a study of Japanese university students suffering from atopic dermatitis, symptoms were classified as follows: 72.7% light, 21.9% moderate, 4.2% severe, and 1.3% extremely severe (Yamamoto and Kawano, 2006). Assuming that the guidelines are designed with the average patient in mind, the focus will thus likely rest on atopic dermatitis patients with light symptoms.

The problem with standard treatment is that it may not always be effective for the small minority of atopic dermatitis patients whose symptoms are severe or extremely severe. I found in the interviews that there are cases in which steroids lose their effectiveness such that their potency must be increased, but the guidelines do not even allude to this subject. The fact that topical steroids have no effect for some patients has also been shown in the research of Furue et al. In a study of 1,271 atopic dermatitis patients, Furue and his team (2003) carried out steroid-based treatment for six months and measured its efficacy. They found that the majority of patients were able to control their symptoms, but for 7% of infants, 10% of children, and 19% of adults, no improvement could be observed in severe and extremely severe cases, no matter how high the potency of the topical steroids. The results of this study suggest that the problem with the aforementioned standard treatment applies to some 20% of adults. It could also be inferred from the data that the older the patients get, the less effective steroids become. Although the study did not detail how long and to what extent patients had used topical steroids, it is not unreasonable to assume that those over a certain age with severe and extremely severe symptoms would have used a substantial amount of topical steroids. While the study does not provide such evidence, it is possible to surmise that the longer patients continue using steroids, the less effect the treatment will have.

The guidelines contain the following information related to duration of use:

> It is highly exceptional for doses as high as 5 to 10 grams of topical steroids to be used continually for more than three months, but it is necessary to perform regular checkups in such cases to assess any systemic impact.

Suitable measures should be considered on a per-patient basis, making an effort to reduce the dose of topical steroids where possible.

(Furue et al., 2009: 1525)

Although a period of three months is mentioned, there were patients in the interviews who had continued using steroids for years or decades, and they experienced first-hand how steroids could gradually become less effective. The guidelines refer to these patients as exceptional, but it can be inferred from the interviews, and the research of Furue's team, that there are actually a large number of such patients. There are patients forced to use steroids long-term while gradually increasing their potency, and it could be seen as a problem that this fact is overlooked in the guidelines.

The subject of steroids becoming less effective over time was not broached in the guidelines of the Japanese Dermatological Association until they were revised in 2016. The phenomenon of the effect of medication weakening after a period of use is called tachyphylaxis, and it is discussed as follows:

During treatment with topical steroids, symptoms that have abated can become exacerbated again. Some suggest that this phenomenon is caused by a rapid decrease in the effectiveness (tachyphylaxis) of topical steroids through long-term use. According to studies of histamine-induced wheal suppression by steroids, the effectiveness of suppression decreased on fourteenth day, and this decrease was seen earlier in dermatitis skin compared to normal skin. However, these studies focused on steroids' suppression of histamine effects, and they are not applicable to atopic dermatitis, since the clinical condition of AD is defined not only by histamine but also by other mechanisms… It is also important to confirm that the medication has actually been applied properly when treatment of dermatitis seems ineffective.

(Katō et al., 2016: 129–130)

Until this revised edition was published in 2016, tachyphylaxis was not even mentioned in the guidelines of the Japanese Dermatological Association, and even in this edition, it is suggested that the reason steroids do not seem to work effectively is not due to tachyphylaxis but due to inappropriate use of steroids.

In fact, a more common stance among doctors is to deny the idea that steroids lose their effectiveness with time. For example, outspoken dermatologist of the Japanese Dermatological Association Kazuhiko Takehara (2000) and a standard treatment-based self-help group NPO called Japan Allergy Tomono Kai are adamant that there are no instances of steroids losing their effectiveness.

Moreover, most doctors also deny the possibility of rebounds or withdrawal symptoms regarding steroids, and the guidelines of the Japanese Dermatological Association do not touch on the topic. Dr. Takehara (2000) asserts that the relapse which occurs after patients stop using steroids is not a rebound, but an exacerbation of the original symptoms. He explains that if patients use appropriate amounts of steroids before stopping using them, even this exacerbation will not occur. He claims that many patients stop using steroids before they have fully recovered from the original symptoms and that is the reason why patients experience this exacerbation of symptoms and feel that it is rebound.

The fact that the negative aspects of steroid treatment, such as decreasing effectiveness over time and rebounds, are denied or ignored seems problematic. This attitude is seen among doctors not only in Japan but also in other countries. However, since the 2010s, the situation has been changing in English-speaking countries, especially in the USA. In 2012, the self-help group International Topical Steroid Addiction Network (ITSAN) was established by patients in order to prevent and treat steroid addiction and withdrawal. They claim that steroids' gradual loss of effectiveness and withdrawal symptoms are caused by the long-term use of steroids, and they therefore encourage patients to stop using them. The idea of steroid addiction has gradually spread among patients in English-speaking countries, and in order to respond to the growing presence of social media addressing this topic, the *Journal of American Academy of Dermatology* published a systematic review of steroid addiction/withdrawal (Hajar et al., 2015). In this review, the authors stated that withdrawal is an adverse effect that generally occurs after inappropriately prolonged and frequent use of high-potency steroids, and they concluded that there is not yet enough evidence to understand and define steroid addiction/withdrawal. As such, the authors recommend that steroids still be seen as key to the successful management of atopic dermatitis. Even though this review ultimately supports the current steroid treatment, it is clear that awareness about steroid addiction/withdrawal has spread among patients, and the situation may be gradually changing.

### Standard treatment advocates' criticism of the Atopy Business and steroid withdrawal treatment

Standard treatment advocates' reluctance to acknowledge the risks of using steroids, such as rebounds and declining effectiveness, has been raised as a concern about standard treatment, but from a standard treatment perspective, the other forms of treatment—particularly steroid withdrawal treatment—have their own serious problems. In this section, some criticisms of these alternative treatments will be introduced. When multiple forms of treatment exist alongside each other, the relationship between them can be hostile as well as supportive, depending on the era and situation. The examples that follow attempt to convey some sense of the hostile relationship between standard treatment and steroid withdrawal treatment.

The most outspoken critic of steroid withdrawal treatment is the aforementioned Kazuhiko Takehara, a dermatology professor in the medical faculty at Kanazawa University and the head of the Japanese Dermatological Association's investigative committee for harm caused by inappropriate atopic dermatitis treatment. Takehara published a book titled *The Atopy Business*, in which he harshly criticized all forms of treatment other than standard treatment. Takehara (2000: 97) defines Atopy Business as 'any commercial business activity targeted toward and contributing to the treatment of atopic dermatitis which is not covered by medical insurance.' It thus clearly refers to products and services provided by businesses outside of the health care system, from water therapy and health foods to beauty treatments, but Takehara (2000: 97) also criticizes as Atopy Business even certain 'treatment carried out and supported by the health care system and doctors.' This highlights the fact that the line between doctor's treatments not covered by medical insurance and alternative medicine is not a clearly defined one.

In his book, Takehara (2000) analyses the tactics used by the Atopy Business, and there are several points of particular interest here. First, unlike pharmaceutical products, health foods and cosmetics do not require any especially stringent testing, and misleading advertising can go unpunished. Second, since remission of atopic dermatitis can occur naturally, the Atopy Business can claim to have cured these cases. Regardless of the treatment, some cases of remission are inevitable, and these patients will believe they have the treatment to thank. Third, even if patients react badly to treatment, the potential excuses are not hard to imagine: 'You're just rebounding from the steroids,' 'You're going through a detox, and it's best to get it all out,' or 'It looks bad now, but this is the turning point of your recovery.' Fourth, patients' expectations have been raised by advertising in the media and elsewhere. Psychologically, the higher the monetary cost to patients, and the higher their physical cost and time commitment, the more likely they are to be convinced that the treatment will be effective, which again raises their hopes for recovery. Further, while inciting fear around the dangers of steroids, there have been cases in which steroids were still actually part of the alternative treatment.

Takehara (2000) lambasts the Atopy Business in this way throughout his analysis. Much of his criticism applies to alternative medicine in its many forms, and much centres on business practices. However, according to Takehara's (2000) own investigation into inappropriate treatment, conducted with 11 departments of dermatology from university hospitals in 1998, the majority of this treatment was not carried out by commercial forms of alternative medicine, but by the health care system itself. Of the 140 cases of inappropriate treatment, as judged by Takehara's criteria, 33% were special forms of treatment under the health care system, and 30% were steroid withdrawal treatment under the health care system. Together, these made up more than half of all cases. The remainder included health foods, other steroid withdrawal treatments, cosmetics, and water therapy.

To reiterate, according to Takehara, any treatment not covered by medical insurance is included in the definition of the Atopy Business. However, while this definition attempts to dismiss all forms of treatment that go against steroids as commercial activities, the author's own investigation showed that steroid withdrawal doctors were actually carrying out treatments covered by medical insurance, not for commercial gain. It is worth noting that Takehara's *inappropriate treatment* category could potentially include a significant number of such cases.

Some of Takehara's criticism of the Atopy Business was directed at steroid withdrawal doctors, but unlike his criticism that was aimed at the wider Atopy Business, the focus of this criticism was the difference in opinion regarding the risks of steroids. Takehara (2000: 159) first counters the argument that steroids become less effective the more they are used:

> All patients admitted to my hospital for atopic dermatitis gained relief from their symptoms within two weeks to at most one month of topical steroid treatment, and were subsequently released. … Patients who followed instructions on how to apply topical steroids correctly saw improvements in their rashes without a single exception.

Takehara believes that any cases of steroids failing to work are the result of problems with the prescription or application, such as inadequate dosing or potency.

The premise of steroid withdrawal treatment is that steroids exacerbate atopic dermatitis and that the symptoms will subside when patients discontinue their use. Takehara (2000) counters, however, that stopping topical steroids does not cure atopic dermatitis itself, but simply relieves one of the side effects of steroids called rosacea-like dermatitis, which includes symptoms such as the reddening of the face, burning sensations, and blemishes.

Another point of criticism from Takehara (2000) is that steroid withdrawal treatment has no established methodology capable of controlling the inflammation of atopic dermatitis after topical steroids are discontinued. The aim of standard treatment is to avoid severe exacerbations of symptoms and maintain patients' quality of life (QOL) while they live with the disease. As a result, steroid withdrawal treatment's approach of forcing patients to endure rebounds that they have no means of avoiding can be seen as going against this goal of standard treatment. The differences between the two forms of treatment are well reflected in their approaches to controlling the severity of symptoms.

Having seen patients with a baseless fear of steroids run to the Atopy Business and exacerbate their symptoms, Takehara (2000: 164) makes his distaste towards steroid withdrawal treatment clear:

> It's no exaggeration to say that we have to clean up the mess left by steroid withdrawal treatment, which lacks any kind of scientific basis.

This attitude reflects the hostility that dermatologists who practise and advocate standard treatment hold towards steroid withdrawal doctors.

Next, to provide a better picture of what patients experience when they undergo standard treatment, two case study patients will be introduced. The first, Kōji (21, male), is an atopic dermatitis patient with relatively mild symptoms. As the study mentioned previously found that 72.7% of Japanese atopic dermatitis patients (university students) have mild symptoms, Kōji could be seen as an example of a patient in the majority. The second patient, Sakie (30, female), on the other hand, has a relatively severe case of atopic dermatitis. Patients with severe and extremely severe symptoms (university students) made up just 5.5% of the total, and a small number overall, but these patients suffer problems all the more.

[Case Study] Kōji (21, male): 'It's really more my constitution than a disease. It just feels natural.'

Kōji's skin appeared so healthy that it was not even apparent that he suffered from atopic dermatitis. At the time, he was a university student and was often in contact with me, though I had no idea he suffered from the disease until he mentioned it. He could be seen as the typical example of an adult atopic dermatitis patient. By using steroids in accordance with standard treatment, he is able to relieve his symptoms and go about his daily life without any obstacles. He trusts his doctor and has not been drawn towards any questionable alternative treatments. While he is not keen on using steroids, he sees them as necessary.

I guess it wasn't so bad from when I was five or six until third or fourth grade in elementary school, but I don't remember clearly. When I started studying for my junior high school entrance exam, it came back, and I haven't recovered from it since then. It's been the same the whole time. When I see the doctor, I get steroids when it's bad. It gets better within a week, and then I give the medication back. When it's okay, it's okay for a while, and when it's bad, that's it. After the symptoms go, I can stop using the medication, and it repeats over like that. With the doctor, it's really just that cycle on repeat. The stronger the medication is the worse it gets, so I have to keep using weaker ones and stopping. I'm on it and off it over and over again. I don't like it, but I don't have a choice. I don't have a choice, but, y'know, I really don't think there's any way of curing it completely, so I don't go trying anything funny.

Kōji is constantly aware of the fact that he has atopic dermatitis, and he sees himself as living his life while controlling his symptoms with steroids. For him, atopic dermatitis is not something he aims to cure, but a natural condition he must continue to live with.

When I noticed my atopic dermatitis, I already had it, so I guess it's like people with poor eyesight wearing glasses. ... It's not like it's because there's some kind of bacteria in your body the whole time. I feel like it's more of a natural thing. It's really more my constitution than a disease. It just feels natural.

In standard treatment, atopic dermatitis is not seen as something that should be cured, and the goal of treatment is to allow patients to go about their daily lives unaffected while controlling the disease with steroids. As Kōji says, atopic dermatitis can be seen as a natural condition that patients must live with, rather than a disease that must be cured. Most atopic dermatitis patients with mild symptoms likely live with the disease while controlling their symptoms, but how does this differ from severe cases? The case of Sakie (30, female) gives some insight into this.

> [Case Study] Sakie (30, female): 'I feel like the number of bad days increases every year.'

Sakie and I met in Japan through Atopicco Network for Children of the Earth. We are both heavily involved in this group. We meet regularly throughout the year at the monthly patient meetings and at yearly summer camps as volunteers, as well as at spring festivals, barbecues, New Year's celebrations, end-of-year parties, and dinners. Sakie works as a carer, and she manages to attend many of the events despite her irregular schedule with a mixture of day shifts and night shifts. She used to do kendo and has confidence in her physical ability. However, she suffers from not only atopic dermatitis, but also asthma and hay fever, and the resulting symptoms mean her body is not always as capable as she would like. Partly because Sakie works at a hospital herself as a carer, she places her trust in doctors and accepts her treatment. As a result, she never tries any forms of alternative medicine, and has stuck with standard treatment while living with her illness. One interview with Sakie was carried out in 2008, and a further two in 2010.

Sakie's atopic dermatitis symptoms first became apparent when she was in junior college. In her second year, the campus was 1 hour and 45 minutes from her home, and the fatigue from the stressful commute and her part-time job led to her developing hay fever. The hay fever caused her face to swell, and there were times when it progressed to allergic rhinitis and allergic conjunctivitis. Medicine had no effect on the rhinitis, and she had to carry five to ten packs of tissues around with her. Her conjunctivitis was also serious, severely affecting her eyesight. She has since had to take anti-allergy medication daily to suppress her rhinitis, conjunctivitis, and asthma.

While in junior college, Sakie was accepted as a third-year university student, and her new campus was even further away. Her new two-hour commute made her condition even worse, and while still in her third year that summer, she was hospitalized when steroid nasal drops, anti-allergy medication, and oral steroids were unable to control her allergy symptoms. She later had nasal laser surgery twice, as well as hyposensitization therapy, but neither seemed to have much of an effect, and her symptoms remain much the same.

Sakie found a job after graduating from university, but after three months, things were not working out for her, and she decided to quit. Just 20 days later, she found a new job as a carer and started work right away. Her allergy symptoms were terrible, but Sakie enjoyed doing kendo, spending time at the sports club, and going out, so she carried on doing these things while taking her medication.

When things were good, I felt healthy, and I'd even go out straight after working a night shift. People who don't use medicine would probably look down on me for this, but if I was just a little bad, at least I had my medicine, so I felt I could just use it if something did happen. I was pretty reckless like that.

When Sakie was 25, however, she developed asthma, and it became harder and harder to be 'reckless' like this. In fact, if Sakie did not control her symptoms with medication, she became unable to function. She had to take different medications for hay fever, asthma, and atopic dermatitis in no small amounts to maintain her condition. When Sakie was 28, during her 2008 interview, she was using moisturizing cream, two types of anti-allergy medication, tablets for asthma, two types of asthma inhalers, Protopic ointment, Antebate ointment (strength class two of five, potent), and Locoid ointment (strength class four, mild), and if her condition worsened, she took oral steroids. Her weakened skin made her susceptible to ringworm and herpes infections. When her conjunctivitis flared up, it could be so bad that she had to take immunosuppressive drugs. In the spring of that year, she said her hay fever gave her a temperature of 39 degrees, but herbal medicine helped to control it after the antipyretics she was prescribed failed to. At the time of this interview, she was not able to eat properly and had lost ten kilogrammes.

A few months after the first interview, in the winter, Sakie's atopic dermatitis became so bad that she was hospitalized for eight days. She had to take ciclosporin to control her symptoms, but she recovered in the new year and was able to return to work. Some time later, she moved to a new hospital and was working there as a carer during the two 2010 interviews. However, her body was in poor condition, and she spoke of the anxiety she felt about continuing the job in the future.

> I don't think my body is going to hold out, so I worry what will happen if this job becomes too hard and I'm not able to do it. I'm not confident that I can keep it up until I'm 65 .... It's getting tougher each year.

The source of this anxiety is her concern about the increasing lack of control she has over her condition each year.

> I feel like the number of bad days increases every year. If the bad days keep on continuing, then my job will just become too hard for me.

In Sakie's case, she is constantly on medication, and if she stops, then her condition declines, so she has no choice but to continue.

> One time I tried to be defiant. I said I didn't need my medication when I felt so good, and I stopped taking it. It was when I felt great and had no problems at all. I stopped taking my medication, but then I felt so awful.

My doctor told me that I had to use medication, that the medication worked and I needed to understand that. Even so, I still didn't get as bad as I do now, since that was years ago.

Since Sakie has to continue taking medication, and the potency is already so high, she lives with the fear that if her condition becomes worse, there will not be anywhere else left to go. She had a relapse just before the second interview, and even an increased dose of oral steroids had no effect.

When I first started oral steroids, I was on prednisolone. I was in a right state. I was taking the prednisolone, but I wasn't getting better. We tried upping the dose a little, but it had absolutely no effect. Whether I rubbed in the steroid cream every day or not, I ended up like that.... I was already using the highest strength in the first place, so it couldn't be raised. So, when things flare up, while other people might be able to increase the potency, I'm just not at that level anymore.

Part of the reason for Sakie using such strong medication is her need to suppress her symptoms so that she is able to work and earn a living for herself. Among the patients who are part of Atopicco Network for Children of the Earth, along with Sakie, a large number believe it is better not to use steroids. Being a part of this group, Sakie feels conflicted knowing that she would not be able to function without taking steroids herself.

When I think about my atopic dermatitis and not using steroids, the first thing that comes to mind is putting bread on the table. If I were in my early 20s, then it might be alright, but I have to think about now and being 28 going on 29. I have a lot of allergies other than atopic dermatitis as well, so I think of myself and how I get. When I think like that, I just can't commit to giving up the medication. I wouldn't really mind dispatch or part-time work, and it's probably the best thing for me, but I can't see making ends meet. ... I have medical bills to pay after all. When I get bad, like if I don't use steroids, then my asthma gets worse, and even if I'm stubborn about not using them, it could be really bad. I can get really bad reactions, and if I don't use them then, I could die. I have to try my best not to end up like that, but I don't have the money to live that kind of life. These kinds of things are always in the back of my mind, and they leave me feeling confused.

From Sakie's story, it is possible to get a sense of the dilemma some patients face of needing to take medication to continue working, while the side effects of the medication continue pushing the body closer to its limits year after year. Sakie followed the standard treatment provided by her doctor strictly, and she is one example of this style of treatment not necessarily leading to any improvement in the patient's condition. As Sakie explained, however, if she does not take her medication, she ends up in an even worse state. When steroids fail to have any effect, her doctor is forced to resort to increasingly stronger options, thus increasing the dose or prescribing more potent medication, such as ciclosporin. In the actual standard treatment guidelines, the protocol, when symptoms flare up, is to use steroids in higher and stronger doses, and then gradually reduce them. What became apparent during Sakie's interview is that actually reducing the dose of steroids can be incredibly difficult. It can be seen from Sakie's story that even following standard treatment to the letter does not necessarily lead to the results described in the guidelines. From these two case studies, it becomes apparent that standard treatment may work well for patients with mild symptoms, who make up the majority, but for patients with severe symptoms, there are also difficult cases that do not conform to the guidelines.

## Steroid withdrawal treatment in Japan

### *What are steroid withdrawal doctors?*

When patients see a doctor in Japan, they typically receive symptomatic treatment centred around steroids in accordance with standard treatment. However, while only a small minority, some dermatologists are concerned about steroid treatment and help patients carry out the so-called steroid withdrawal treatment. These doctors are known among Japanese patients as *steroid withdrawal doctors.* How did these doctors end up following steroid withdrawal treatment when most dermatologists follow standard treatment? How does their explanatory model differ from standard treatment model? What exactly is steroid withdrawal treatment? And what do patients experience when they try it?

The steroid withdrawal doctors themselves can provide some insight into the answers to these questions. I was able to meet a number of steroid withdrawal doctors through the self-help group Atopy-free.com and Atopicco Network for Children of the Earth. The names of these doctors are relatively well-known among atopic dermatitis patients, and those wishing to seek out steroid withdrawal treatment turn to these doctors.

Unlike standard treatment, steroid withdrawal treatment does not have a clear set of guidelines, and it is not something that any doctor could reliably carry out with any consistency. However, since its core aim is to discontinue the use of steroids, steroid withdrawal treatment could in theory be carried out by patients themselves without the help of a doctor. There is no study on patients who stop using steroids without consulting a doctor, but they might be more numerous than those who do. Working together with a doctor, however, comes with an added sense of security; patients then have access to anti-allergy medication or ointments that can suppress symptoms, measures to mitigate any relapses, and proper treatment of any infections that may occur.

Furthermore, since discontinuing steroid treatment requires enduring a terrible relapse, the level of trust required between the patient and doctor is much higher than with standard treatment. In some cases, the biggest reason the doctor is needed in steroid withdrawal treatment could be said to be psychological support and encouragement rather than providing prescriptions. Perhaps for this reason, the bond between steroid withdrawal doctors and their patients is incredibly strong. A small number of these doctors even have a following, with patients helping them prepare seminars and other events. The bond between doctors and patients, as well as among patients themselves, can be seen in the communities patients have formed on social networks such as Mixi and Facebook or through the mailing lists they use to connect with doctors. These bonds often serve as a great source of support when patients have to deal with the severe symptoms of a relapse.

One complaint against standard treatment mentioned several times by interview participants was the way that doctors prescribed steroids almost robotically, without really looking at their symptoms. Steroid withdrawal treatment, on the other hand, can be difficult to continue at all without a solid commitment from the doctor. I was permitted to observe a consultation in 2008 at Yoshioka Skin Clinic (pseudonym), which offers steroid withdrawal treatment. The following are my notes taken during that consultation. They give a sense of the closeness between the doctors and patients.

The morning hours at Yoshioka Skin Clinic are from 9:30 to 12:00, and I sat in on one morning consultation. The consultation room was small and furnished simply with the doctor's desk, a bed, and a chair. A microscope, a PC, and some medical books were on top of the desk. The walls of the room were decorated with many letters and pictures, especially from children, expressing thanks to Dr. Yoshioka. A series of photographs showing an elementary student's procession through steroid withdrawal treatment was displayed prominently in the room. There were five photographs in total: the top one showed the child before beginning treatment, the second showed him two weeks later when his condition was at its worst, the next two showed him four and seven months into treatment with increasingly improved skin, and the final picture showed him a few years later with perfect skin.

Dr. Yoshioka had many atopic dermatitis patients. Of the 40 patients who visited him that morning, 23 suffered with the condition. One of the most intriguing things about the consultations that day came with the 29th patient. A father and mother and their son, a third-grade elementary school student, visited together as a family. It was rare for fathers to attend the clinic. It was their first consultation at Yoshioka Skin Clinic, and the parents had solemn expressions. Their child was suffering with atopic dermatitis and asthma. He had been attending another clinic for a long time and had been using steroids for eight years, since he was assured that it was okay.

The doctor asked the boy to remove his clothes. There were numerous atopic lesions on the boy's body that looked like brown scabs. 'It's said that steroids have no side effects, but the visible veins around the chest area here are a clear side effect,' said the doctor as the parents looked on in silence.

When he asked if they were prepared to attempt steroid withdrawal, the parents said 'yes' as if they had already decided from the start. 'Okay, but there are rules,' he said before instructing the boy directly: 'You'll get up early, you'll walk or run every day, you'll communicate well, you won't play games for more than 30 minutes a day, and you'll appreciate what your parents are doing for you.' He then turned to the parents: 'Use 30% disciplining and 70% comforting. Don't tell him not to scratch.' The mother recorded what he said in a notebook.

The doctor was especially nice to child patients. He told the boy to work hard, become successful, and marry someone as kind as his mother. It was an old habit of his to tell atopic dermatitis patients that they were beautiful, kind, and smart.

Observing the consultation made it clear that these kinds of compliments are effective. If an adolescent boy has lesions on his face, Dr. Yoshioka focuses on praising his intelligence. It is not difficult to imagine how having something like this to cling onto during tougher times can provide great mental support. Receiving such praise from a doctor allows patients some room for optimism, and it can put their minds at rest. It was easy to see why patients speak of how reassuring it is to visit Dr. Yoshioka. The sense of relief when they were told that they would recover from their condition was almost palpable.

Yoshioka Skin Clinic shows, however, just one example of a steroid withdrawal doctor at work. All such doctors do not necessarily carry out consultations in this way. Nevertheless, in my experience of interacting with several steroid withdrawal doctors, it seems that the charisma and closeness with patients displayed by Dr. Yoshioka are common characteristics among them.

### Steroid withdrawal treatment's background

Next, I will examine the reasons behind the emergence of steroid withdrawal treatment in opposition to standard treatment. I was able to interview former dermatologist Dr. Mototsugu Fukaya, who was involved in steroid withdrawal treatment until 2003. Dr. Fukaya became a dermatologist in 1986 and secured a position the following year in the dermatology department of a national hospital, where he continued working until 2003. Around the time Dr. Fukaya began work in 1986, the only people among the public aware of atopic dermatitis were mothers with dry hands and their children. There were very few books on the condition aimed at ordinary people, and even doctors had limited access to information. Back then, Dr. Fukaya learnt from his peers and carried out treatment with topical steroids.

When I worked part-time at a city hospital, we had young children put weak steroids on their face and strong ones on their body. As long as they reacted well to treatment, then that was that, since it was the kind of condition they recovered from as they grew up. Since the mothers had dry hands, they were given Rinderon,[1] and for bad cases Dermovate[2]. That's how I learned to deal with it on the job. Basically, by looking at what the previous doctor had written on the patient's record and continuing to prescribe the same thing, that way of doing things just came naturally.

After working for several years at a national hospital, Dr. Fukaya was put in charge of a ward in the dermatology department. Since it was limited to eight beds at the time, the department thought of employing a method known as educational hospitalization for atopic dermatitis patients to minimize the time and cost of treatment. Educational hospitalization was being used by doctors for diabetes, so they decided to try something along the same lines for atopic dermatitis.

And then adult atopic dermatitis patients started appearing here and there, which was perhaps a result of steroid withdrawal attempts. Things got worse quickly, and patients were asking to be admitted to the hospital or treated some other way. They said the steroids made them better, but getting better that way wasn't what they wanted. I seem to remember experiencing this sometime in the late 80s.

Dr. Fukaya did not want the educational hospitalization for atopic dermatitis to consist only of admitting patients to the hospital; instead, he wanted to draw up some kind of curriculum. At the time, paediatricians at Chiba University were carrying out Isodine treatment, and this was featured on NHK's television pro-gramme *Kenkō Today* (*Health Today*). Dr. Fukaya decided to try it himself, and instructed patients to use Isodine in the morning, afternoon, and evening during their two-week admission. He also collected television programmes and videos aimed at atopic dermatitis patients, and he used his own money to create a small library of books on the topic. This created an environment that allowed patients to learn about the condition while they were undergoing the Isodine treatment.

I thought it would be great if patients could get better safely and comfort-ably. When we allowed patients to register for educational hospitalization, we were inundated with patients who had attempted steroid withdrawal. Looking at this as just an ordinary dermatologist, I couldn't really deny what I was seeing. They quit steroids, went through a relapse, and finally ended up a lot better. So, I'd say it was actually me who learned the most from educational hospitalization, and this was how it started for me.

Through caring for steroid withdrawal patients who attended the educational hospitalization, Dr. Fukaya observed atopic dermatitis symptoms improving af-ter patients stopped using steroids. There are other doctors who began offering steroid withdrawal treatment after observing a similar trend among their own patients.

Fortunately, many steroid withdrawal doctors have published books and detailed what led them to provide such treatment. Doctors Kenji Satō (2008) and Akiharu Tamaki (2008) exemplify this in their books. Both doctors provided standard treatment before feeling its limitations and turning to steroid withdrawal treatment in the hope of bettering the situation. Dr. Tamaki (2008: 10–11) explains in this excerpt from his book how he originally got into steroid withdrawal treatment.

> Towards the end of the 1980s, there was some resistance against treatment using steroid ointment. There were cases of people not improving no matter how much they used, and a large number of cases of a side effect referred to as red demon face. I felt that continuing steroid treatment as we were couldn't guarantee remission. Stopping steroids leads to temporary withdrawal symptoms, but I believed they would settle down. The basis for my belief was in the treatment of rosacea-like dermatitis (perioral dermatitis), a side effect of steroid ointments, which involved discontinuing steroid ointments, and was well known for doing so. When stopping the ointments, patients would experience a relapse, and their symptoms appeared to worsen temporarily. However, it was already known by the end of the 1970s that this would settle down sometime between two and six months later. ... By the 1990s, there were patients who didn't want to use steroids at all. I would explain to them as follows: When you stop using steroids, you'll experience a relapse of dermatitis, and perhaps even a temporary exacerbation. It could be thought that these symptoms may heal as with rosacea-like dermatitis, but it's also possible that the atopy symptoms will not heal at all. Since this is a method that nobody else has tried, I don't really know how things will play out. Patients would show their resolve and tell me that they didn't mind, and that they wanted to try treatment without steroids. In the beginning, patients would be admitted to hospital to carry out treatment without steroids.

The background of Dr. Satō's (2008: 11–12) decision to provide steroid withdrawal treatment provides an additional example.

> The majority of infants sent to me who 'wouldn't get better' were recognized as having side effects of topical steroids, including atrophy of the skin, dilated capillaries, and erythema. I instructed any patient with a history of topical steroid use to discontinue their medication, and there would be a temporary flare-up of skin rashes, but in the majority of cases a big improvement could be observed before long.
>
> While experiencing these events, I was referred a two-year-old infant who had been diagnosed with plaque psoriasis. There were no silver-grey scales anywhere on his body, so I judged it not to be plaque psoriasis. He had

severely inhibited growth for his age, and was very short and underweight. Topical steroids were being absorbed across his whole body, and I judged that the suppression of his adrenal glands was leading to his inhibited growth. I took him off steroids and prescribed Azunol ointment.

After a while, the severe scaling on his skin disappeared, but skin across his body remained red. The family went to see a new doctor after moving, who had them stop the Azunol ointment, and the redness went away and the boy's growth returned to normal. From this case, I saw that the severe side effects of long-term topical steroid use could also be cured by steroid withdrawal. I also felt it strange that after stopping the steroids and using Azunol ointment the redness remained, but then all skin rashes disappeared when stopping that. This is how my own steroid withdrawal treatment began.

In the case of all three of the doctors, they speak from experience of an increasing number of patients whose symptoms could not be treated by steroids, and how stopping steroids and other ointments led to a relapse before an improvement in symptoms. Their treatment did not follow the guidelines, and they relied on their experience over mainstream methods. It no doubt required a great amount of determination to trust their own experience and change the form of their treatment.

What must not be overlooked is that steroid withdrawal was not something that originated with steroid withdrawal doctors, but rather with patients themselves. The patients showed the desire to stop using steroids, and it was only after they went through with it that steroid withdrawal doctors were able to notice improvement in their symptoms. After that, each doctor applied trial and error in an effort to establish a form of steroid withdrawal treatment. When carrying out treatment without using powerful anti-inflammatories like steroids, all they could do was observe their patients' reactions. In this sense, steroid withdrawal treatment contrasts with steroid treatment in the way doctors work very closely together with the patient. As such, it is possible to say that steroid withdrawal treatment is a form of treatment that involves the participation of the patient.

### *Treatment goals and explanatory models of steroid withdrawal doctors*

Put simply, the goal of the treatment that steroid withdrawal doctors provide is to cure atopic dermatitis. In his book, steroid withdrawal doctor Shigeki Fujisawa (2004: 14) speaks of the possibility of curing atopic dermatitis and writes in a way that provides patients with encouragement:

Atopic dermatitis is currently thought of as a disease that is difficult to treat. It is precisely for this reason that symptomatic treatment is not the answer. Doctors should encourage lifestyle improvements and continue to provide curative treatment, which can enhance the patient's natural ability to heal, until finally the day of a cure arrives.

Both steroid withdrawal doctors and alternative medicine view atopic dermatitis as a curable disease and set a complete cure as the goal of treatment. However, the explanatory model of atopic dermatitis treatment provided by steroid withdrawal doctors differs from that of alternative medicine. Steroid withdrawal doctors do not subscribe to the idea that steroids accumulate in the body and need to be expelled, which forms the explanatory model of alternative medicine. Instead, they approach steroid withdrawal from a more medical and scientific perspective.

What separates the explanatory model of steroid withdrawal treatment from that of standard treatment is the acknowledgement that long-term topical steroid use can make atopic dermatitis increasingly difficult to treat. One steroid withdrawal doctor who is attempting to verify this theory scientifically is Mototsugu Fukaya. In his book, referencing studies on steroid addiction by doctors such as A. M. Kligman and M. J. Cork, Dr. Fukaya (2010) explains steroid addiction scientifically. According to Cork, using topical steroids is effective when severe inflammation of the skin occurs, but long-term continuous use has the effect of breaking down the barrier function of the skin. As a result, allergens are able to enter the skin more easily and potentially exacerbate the atopic dermatitis. When this happens, applying steroids will provide relief, but the symptoms return even faster when not applied, leading to a viscous cycle. This state is referred to as steroid addiction (Fukaya et al., 2014).

The core difference between the explanatory models of standard treatment and steroid withdrawal treatment lies in whether steroid addiction is acknowledged to exist or not. Within the guidelines of standard treatment, it is recommended that the dose of steroids be gradually lowered until medication can ultimately be stopped completely. This is because steroid addiction is not believed to exist, and thus lowering the dose of steroids will not lead to a relapse. However, if it were possible to become dependent on steroids and stopping them did lead to a relapse, then carrying out treatment according to the guidelines would be difficult in practice. Referencing Shōtaro Harada's study on the effect of gradually lowering the potency of steroids on atopic dermatitis patients, Dr. Fukaya points out that there were a constant number of patients who experienced an exacerbation at some point during this process. According to Dr. Fukaya (2010), regardless of the measures taken, around 24% of patients are able to stop using steroids without relapsing, but reducing the potency or outright stopping the use of steroids leads to a relapse for all other patients. Standard treatment guidelines dictate that any relapse must be dealt with by increasing the potency of steroids once again in order to control the symptoms. As a result, patients are never able to fully stop using steroids.

There are very few doctors in the world who believe in the existence of steroid addiction. However, American dermatologists Marvin J. Rapaport and Mark Lebwoh (2003) have published a study on steroid addiction and relapses which reported that 87 of his 100 patients were able to recover from atopic dermatitis by stopping the use of steroids. Furthermore, the steroid withdrawal doctors

I know of exchange information about their treatment attempts, and it could be said that they share a similar explanatory model.

### Treatment methods

The approach of steroid withdrawal doctors to treatment is essentially to stop the use of steroid medication, and it does not really go far beyond this. While alternative medicine practitioners similarly aim to stop steroid use, they also recommend various other forms of treatment, including hot spring therapy, topical medication other than steroids, drinking aloe vera juice, and taking supplements. This is because selling treatment products is a key source of income for such practitioners. In contrast, the steroid withdrawal doctors I met did not appear to be involved in such treatment for the sake of making money. They did, however, offer treatments such as anti-allergy medication to relieve itchiness, non-steroid creams and ointments to suppress inflammation, and ultraviolet light therapy in order to help patients stopping the use of steroids better endure their relapses, but these were all reasonable treatments covered by insurance. In its simplest form, steroid withdrawal treatment can be summarized as stopping steroids and waiting for a period of time until the relapse is over.

Next, it is helpful to examine some of the forms of this palliative treatment recommended by steroid withdrawal doctors. Dr. Fujisawa recommends what he terms ointment withdrawal along with steroid withdrawal, which refers to stopping the use of ointments in order to allow the skin to regain its ability to produce moisture. However, when providing treatment in practice, he prescribes pine tar ointment, and is not especially dogmatic about ointment withdrawal. Dr. Fujisawa (2004) additionally recommends lifestyle improvements such as stress management and cutting down on oils containing linoleic acid while increasing intake of alpha-linolenic acid, as well as things like hot baths. As natural forms of treatment, steroid withdrawal doctor Tamaki (2008) recommends developing habits such as getting up and going to bed early and eating regular meals. Another steroid withdrawal doctor, Satō (2008), gives similar advice to that of Dr. Fujisawa and recommends what he terms moisturizer withdrawal, which refers to gradually using less moisturizer to allow the skin to moisturize itself. He additionally suggests restricting fluids and using diuretics to relieve weeping wound symptoms, warns against wiping secretions from the skin or picking scabs during the relapse, and recommends regular exercise, avoiding late nights, and eating at regular intervals.

As described earlier, the treatment provided by steroid withdrawal doctors differs subtly by doctor, but withdrawing from steroid use and improving lifestyle factors form a common basis. Dr. Fukaya (1999: 4) sums up the treatment methods this way:

> Although it may be hard to understand, there is almost no medication or 'treatment'. Patients just come to my office, undress and have their picture taken, have a chat, and go home. I can't count the number of times patients

have said something like, 'It's funny, but the day I come to your office I feel I recover just a little.' In other words, the role of doctors in steroid withdrawal is no more or no less than that.

Since steroid withdrawal treatment is, as Dr. Fukaya says, essentially giving up steroids, it is rarely something that doctors can manage by prescribing medication. However, the significance of the peace of mind given by a doctor's support should not be underestimated.

### Criticism against standard treatment and alternative medicine

This section will take a look at how steroid withdrawal doctors engage with groups in the other sectors. In the same way that standard treatment is critical of alternative medicine and steroid withdrawal doctors, these doctors are also critical of standard treatment and alternative medicine, and their criticism of standard treatment is especially fierce.

The following excerpt from Dr. Fukaya's book expresses the level of hostility steroid withdrawal doctors feel towards standard treatment. Dr. Fukaya (2010: 31) speaks here of the anguish he felt while working as a dermatologist:

> I'm sorry if it sounds like I'm complaining, but that time (when I was engaged in steroid withdrawal treatment in the 1990s) was incredibly tough. Nevertheless, I was serious about consulting patients with 'steroid addiction', having them overcome it and reporting my findings officially. If I could have done that, it would have become scientific fact, and the medical community would have eventually understood it. Dermatology consultations, or rather the way topical steroids were viewed, would have changed, and this would likely have been reflected in the guidelines. If this could have happened, I would have had things easier too. That's how I was thinking. My mind and body couldn't survive it. I became depressed and lost faith in dermatology. … I suffered with insomnia, damaged my health and wellbeing, and eventually reached my limits, which is when I decided to quit. If I had made an error due to fatigue, the repercussions would have hit the name of steroid withdrawal as hard as they would have hit me, and that's one thing I couldn't bear to see.

As Dr. Fukaya writes, the source of the anger that steroid withdrawal doctors feel is the continued refusal of doctors who push standard treatment to recognize steroid addiction, that is, the diminishing returns of steroid medication and existence of a relapse when stopping treatment. Doctors who carry out steroid withdrawal treatment have, as discussed, noticed steroid addiction in clinical practice and did not learn of it in medical school or from textbooks. Within what one might call orthodox medical education and treatment, side effects such as steroid addiction are not taken seriously, and the small number of doctors who have noticed these side effects is left fighting against the orthodoxy of the standard treatment guidelines.

Dr. Fukaya (2010) has, for instance, submitted a formal request to the Japanese Dermatological Association to have the guidelines take note of steroid addiction and relapses. In his book, Dr. Tamaki (2008) also criticizes the lack of any mention in the guidelines of how steroid use could eventually be stopped at any point. Dr. Satō (2008) has similarly criticized the guidelines in his writing and has offered a draft revision that would avoid steroid use.

In addition to their criticism of standard treatment, Dr. Tamaki (2008) and Dr. Satō (2008) have also criticized alternative medicine in their writing. Both mention the lack of evidence for its efficacy and raise the example of herbal medicine as something that should not be used, since it has side effects, despite the common belief otherwise. Both standard treatment and alternative medicine thus come under fire, and steroid withdrawal doctors could be seen as positioning themselves as different from both.

[Case Study] Yoshimi (40, female): 'Who cares if you have a rash? That's what I think. Maybe people overthink things.'

In this section, Yoshimi's story will be introduced as a case study of a patient who has received treatment from a steroid withdrawal doctor. I first met Yoshimi at the Atopy Forum, an event held by the self-help group Atopy-free.com at Toyotomi Hot Spring in Hokkaido, Japan. The event allowed patients to enjoy hot spring therapy while exchanging opinions and hearing lectures from a dermatologist. I was approached by Yoshimi at the event, and we have been in contact ever since.

Yoshimi was in the middle of a relapse at the Atopy Forum but has since overcome it. She is happily married with two young children. She has experience working as a staff member for a patient community group organized by steroid withdrawal doctor Dr. Yoshioka, who treated her atopic dermatitis, and she is in favour of steroid withdrawal. I interviewed Yoshimi once in 2007, twice in 2010, via e-mail in 2013, and again in person in 2014.

Yoshimi suffered from atopic dermatitis from childhood, and she was able to control her symptoms to some extent by applying topical steroids. From elementary school until her first year of high school, she was a bright and active student, but as a possible result of bullying, her atopic dermatitis began to worsen in her second year. Despite violence from her father at home, and rarely leaving the house in her third year, she managed to attend high school enough to graduate. For two years or so after graduation, Yoshimi felt emotionally unstable and spent many late nights out on the town. Before long, she decided to give up that lifestyle and got a part-time job at a bar. Although topical steroids relieved her atopic dermatitis symptoms to some extent, they were still visible all over her body. It was tough for her, but her boss looked out for her, and she was able to work in a comfortable environment.

After working at the bar for around a year, she worked other part-time jobs at bars and cafes. With the money she saved, she managed to become a certified draftsperson and started doing dispatch work tracing technical diagrams at architecture firms and electronics companies. However, Yoshimi developed cataracts after some time, so she had to give up working on diagrams because of her vision. Her atopic dermatitis flared up due to the stress in her personal life when she was 25, but she controlled the symptoms with steroids. She went through jobs as a telephone operator and editor, and even returned to the bars she had worked at previously.

When she was around 28, Yoshimi was forced to use increasingly potent topical steroids to keep her symptoms under control, and ultimately had to use medication from the most potent class. Her doctor gently persuaded her that it would be okay, so she used them without any misgivings, assuming there was little other choice. However, sudden exacerbations became increasingly frequent even when using her medication, and she came across Dr. Yoshioka when deciding to change clinics. This was when she was 32, which was a year after she met the man who became her husband.

At Yoshioka Skin Clinic, Yoshimi was prescribed pine tar ointment and low-potency topical steroids. Since she had been using such potent topical steroids before then, switching to a lower potency caused a sudden exacerbation of her symptoms. Her symptoms became so severe that she was not even able to stand, so she was forced to quit her job. At the time, while still wearing her pyjamas, she had her boyfriend help her into a taxi to her office, and her boss came out to the taxi so that she could take care of her resignation documents.

Yoshimi's strength is in her refusal to give up even when her symptoms are at their worst. She had been going to dance classes for a year before her first visit to Yoshioka Skin Clinic, and she had a stage performance planned just when she experienced a flare up in her symptoms. Initially, she decided not to take part in the performance, but her teacher reassured her and helped her hide the symptoms with makeup. Her symptoms were so bad she was practically bedridden before this, but a week before the performance, she practised the routine relentlessly and was able to dance when the day came. Her dance teacher and classmates are people she holds incredibly dear.

Despite her positivity, Yoshimi experienced another severe relapse some time after her dance performance and was hospitalized due to the gastroenteritis that accompanied it. When she got out of hospital, she had stopped using steroids completely, and her relapse continued for several months before the symptoms gradually started to improve. When Yoshimi was 35, she married the man she had been dating, and became pregnant two years later. Before her pregnancy, her atopic dermatitis symptoms had good days and bad days, but the severity decreased over time, and she showed a great improvement by the time she was pregnant. After giving birth, she was able to maintain a relatively symptomless state for some time. When interviewed in 2010, Yoshimi had symptoms on her fingers, and spoke of itchiness when trying to sleep, but judging from her face and general appearance, it was not readily apparent that she suffered from atopic dermatitis.

Yoshimi gave birth to her second child in 2012. After the baby was born, she suffered from insomnia and her symptoms worsened. When contacted in 2013, her condition had deteriorated again. However, she showed characteristic strength in continuing to do the things she wanted to do without being perturbed by her atopic dermatitis. That strength could also be seen when, despite the severity of her symptoms, she took to the stage to dance. When I first interviewed Yoshimi, she had visible symptoms, but when asked if she thought her atopic dermatitis could be cured, she answered as follows:

> When it comes to what a cure means to me, I really think it's something that depends on the person. I kind of think that, in my current condition, I'm already on the way to a full recovery.

I then asked when she feels most aware of having atopic dermatitis.

> Well, I don't really think about it. I tend to just think: 'So what if I have a rash?' … I think that maybe people overthink it. When other people see it, maybe they think it might be dermatitis, and they're welcome to think that. I don't actually think other people think that though. Everyone has their own problems, right? I don't think they really look. I think there are a lot of people who may see something on my face, but don't really know the difference between spots and dermatitis.

By not allowing her atopic dermatitis to get her down, Yoshimi is able to get on with her life without worrying. I asked if her attitude had changed compared to the past.

> I really think meeting Dr. Yoshioka was a big thing for me. And also having my husband there for me. Having these people around me has been really important to me.

Yoshimi has people around her who understand and support her, including her husband, siblings, and friends, and building close relationships with these people could be seen as a significant factor. Atopic dermatitis is often dismissed as just a case of atopy, and it is commonly the case that those around the patient do not understand the disease. It is clear that the people who have overcome this social hardship build close relationships with those around them, and work hard to have those people understand their suffering. It seems that part of Yoshimi's strength also comes from the understanding and support of those close to her.

Another characteristic of Yoshimi's way of thinking is her strong refusal to use topical steroids. When asked how she felt about using topical steroids during an interview in 2010, she rejected the idea frankly, saying such medication was better suited to surgical patients rather than those with atopic dermatitis.

When I contacted her by e-mail in 2013, Yoshimi had softened her stance somewhat. Although she was still against using topical steroids, she had started to feel that people should have a healthy amount of scepticism, rather than believing everything steroid withdrawal doctors say. She was not able to control her own symptoms while undergoing treatment dictated by doctors and others, and more recently, she has started thinking about the problem in her own way. She has been able to take charge of her symptoms herself. For example, when it came to self-help groups, she had trouble admitting that she needed help and felt embarrassed about participating. However, she now feels that doing things that can help her is nothing to be ashamed of. She also now believes that patients who have trouble maintaining their lifestyle without topical steroids are making a valid choice, and she prays that it does not end badly for them.

The problem of whether or not to use topical steroids appears to present two diametrically opposed choices, but when looking at the patient-doctor relationship, many patients who are under either standard treatment or steroid withdrawal treatment follow their doctor's order without question. However, Yoshimi speaks of how she began to have doubts about both kinds of treatment and seems to have gradually found her own perspective.

## The professional sector in the UK

In order to explain the professional sector in the UK, it is necessary to first provide some understanding of the different health care systems in the UK and Japan. The UK has a publicly funded health care system called the NHS, which was founded after the Second World War in 1948. The NHS has been run on the ideal that 'good health care should be available to all, regardless of wealth,' and it therefore provides free health care to all UK citizens. While Japan operates a social insurance system, a combination of insurance fees and government expenditure together with patient contributions, the UK's NHS runs on tax revenues, meaning that the government pays the majority of costs and that patients are not charged medical expenses, even for surgery or childbirth. However, it should be noted that in the NHS, costs related to optical and dental treatment, as well as outpatient prescriptions, have to be partially covered by the patient.

The way patients receive treatment also differs between the Japanese system and the NHS. In Japan, patients can freely choose the clinic or hospital they want to visit, whereas NHS patients must receive treatment from their local general practitioner (GP), who may refer them to a specialized clinic or hospital for further treatment. The GP thus acts as a kind of gatekeeper who connects patients with specialist doctors. My own experience with the NHS is illustrative of how the system works.

While I was in the UK, I registered with the NHS and received NHS treatment during my times of illness. I first had to register with a local NHS clinic and undergo a simple health check-up. When falling ill, I had to make an appointment to see a GP at the local clinic. I found that it was typically possible to make an appointment within a week. However, I knew that during times of emergency, walk-in centres or emergency services were available without any appointment. On the day of the appointment, patients like me would receive a consultation with their GP, and if necessary, they might undergo tests or receive prescriptions. Outpatient prescriptions are not free, so this type of medication would need to be purchased from a pharmacy. However, exemptions are made for those unable to pay, such as children under 16, students aged 16–18, the elderly people, and low-income earners. Although patients are referred to specialist clinics or hospitals when their GP deems it necessary, I did not experience this and was able to receive all my treatment at a local clinic. In fact, the actual number of patients who see specialists make up just 2%–5% of those seen by GPs, and the majority of patients are successfully treated at their local clinic (Takeuchi and Takenoshita, 2009). This is also true for atopic dermatitis treatment; most patients rely only on the primary care of their GP, and it is rare for them to visit dermatology specialists (Scottish Intercollegiate Guidelines Network, 2011).

Although the health care systems differ in Japan and the UK, the general form of modern medical treatment is essentially the same. Modern medical treatment guidelines in the UK can be understood by drawing on those from the British Association of Dermatologists (BAD) and the National Institute for Health and Care Excellence (NICE). NICE is an independent organization based on objective expertise, and it is essentially responsible for determining what treatments and drugs should be used by NHS services. The number of doctors who follow NICE guidelines has risen to around 70%–80%, and those who do not follow them are required to provide an explanation of why they do not.

Just as in Japan, the dominant premise that emerges in the UK guidelines is that there is no curative treatment for atopic dermatitis, and the foundation of treatment aimed at controlling symptoms is moisturizing agents and topical steroids. Regarding these palliative topical steroids, in the UK, they are divided into four classes, mild, moderate, potent, and very potent; meanwhile, there are five classes of such steroids in Japan, mild, moderate, potent, very potent, and most potent. Patients are told which class to use based on the severity of their symptoms and the area of the body, such as the face, arms, or legs. In addition, the guidelines recommend other types of medication to control inflammation, including topical immunosuppressive drugs. In the UK, both tacrolimus ointment and pimecrolimus ointment are sold, whereas only tacrolimus ointment is available in Japan. In both countries, ultraviolet therapy, oral steroids, and the oral immunosuppressive drug ciclosporin are used, and an additional oral immunosuppressive drug called azathioprine is used in the UK.

As further treatment options, antihistamines and herbal medicine are alluded to in both the Japanese and British guidelines. It is additionally recommended to make use of bandages containing a special paste to soothe the affected areas and to administer antibiotics and antiseptics when patients suffer an infection. In both countries, mites, food allergies, and reactions to the cream or ointment itself are believed to trigger symptoms, so caution is advised.

Although the general principles of treatment do not differ significantly between Japan and the UK, one notable difference is in the recommended length of topical steroid treatment. No estimated timeframe is mentioned in the Japanese guidelines, whereas the BAD has a recommended protocol for cases of acute flare-ups. According to the BAD protocol, topical steroids should be applied twice daily for a maximum of 10–14 days, after which it is preferable to observe a rest period when only moisturizing creams are used (National Institute for Clinical Excellence, 2004). However, for chronic flare-ups, topical steroids should be used for four to six weeks until the patient is able to go into remission (Primary Care Dermatology Society & British Association of Dermatologists, 2009). Furthermore, when patients buy topical steroids after receiving a prescription from their doctor, the intended length of use may even be written on the packaging. For example, betamethasone, a potent topical steroid, has the following label on its packaging:

> Apply it sparingly once daily to affected areas for a maximum of 10 days only. Steroid potency, potent.

Since there is no clearly set limit for the number of days topical steroids can be used in Japan, it is common for patients there to be confused about when exactly they should stop using them.

When compared to Japan, there is much more disclosure of information regarding the cost of and evidence supporting treatment and drugs in the UK. This is a result of the UK policies aiming to improve the transparency and quality of treatment outlined in the reforms of the NHS Plan in 2000. *Transparency of treatment* refers to making public all forms of information, from how standards are set and how guidelines are established to how progress is monitored and evaluated. This transparency helps to galvanize the health care system and to obtain feedback from patients.

This transparency of treatment also means the release of details about the cost of treating atopic dermatitis in the UK. The yearly cost of treating atopic dermatitis in the mid-90s was £125 million, the annual personal cost to the population was £297 million, and the annual societal cost due to lost working days was £43 million. These three figures together put the annual cost of atopic dermatitis in the mid-90s UK at £465 million. In addition, £11.6 million was spent on prescriptions for topical steroids in 2002 (Scottish Intercollegiate Guidelines Network, 2011).

Detailed data regarding the evidence supporting treatment is also released in the UK. In 1993, the NHS R&D Health Technology Assessment Programme was set up as part of the National Institute for Health Research (NIHR). As an independent organization, its aim is to investigate the efficacy and cost of treatment, as well as the influence of health technology, and to release the related data. These investigations group treatments into four categories, from those backed by randomized controlled trials (RCT) and reliable evidence to those with no evidence whatsoever. For example, these are some atopic dermatitis treatments in each category:

1   There was reasonable RCT evidence to support the use of oral ciclosporin, topical corticosteroids, psychological approaches, and ultraviolet light therapy.
2   There was insufficient evidence to make recommendation on maternal allergen avoidance for disease prevention, oral antihistamines, Chinese herbs, dietary restriction in established atopic eczema, homeopathy, house dust mite reduction, massage therapy, hypnotherapy, evening primrose oil, emollients, topical coal tar, and topical doxepin.
3   There was no RCT evidence to support any clear clinical benefit on the use of avoidance of enzyme washing powders, cotton clothing as opposed to soft-weave synthetics, biofeedback, twice-daily as opposed to once-daily topical corticosteroids, topical antibiotic/steroid combinations versus topical steroids alone, and antiseptic bath additives.
4   There was complete absence of RCT evidence on short bursts of potent versus longer-term weaker topical steroids, dilution of topical corticosteroids, oral prednisolone and azathioprine, salt baths, impregnated bandages, wet-wrap bandages, water softening devices, allergy testing, and different approaches to organization of care.

The Health Technology Assessment Programme has concluded that, based on the evidence available, there are many limitations regarding the prevention and treatment of atopic dermatitis, including the number of short-term studies on similar treatments, the lack of a common standard for measuring efficacy, the poor quality of reporting in clinical trials, and the lack of data on the problems most important to medical staff and patients (Hoare et al., 2000). It is interesting to note here that the problem of addiction to topical steroids is not dealt with in this report, nor is it at all in the professional sector more broadly in either Japan or the UK.

In its guidelines, NICE recommends the highest possible quality of treatment at the lowest possible cost, based on the available evidence and total cost. As a result, it is the policy of the British government to publicly disclose information and to fund research into treatment which is effective while also keeping costs down. The policies surrounding atopic dermatitis in the professional sectors of Japan and the UK do not differ significantly overall, but with a free health care system and the full disclosure of costs and evidence, differences can be found in the way things are done and in the make-up of the systems in the NHS.

The overall similarity in modern medical treatment in Japan and the UK is reinforced at the level of individual patient experience. Lulu (46, female) will be introduced in more detail in Chapter 5, along with the self-help group called the National Eczema Society, but it is worth noting here that her treatment and experience in the UK is very similar to Sakie's (30, female) experience in Japan, as described in Chapter 1. Lulu sees a dermatology specialist and uses the immunosuppressive drug ciclosporin to control her symptoms. Comparing Sakie's and Lulu's cases, it seems that the treatment and experiences of patients with severe symptoms differ very little between Japan and the UK.

The experiences of patients with lighter symptoms also reveal some similarities. A detailed case study of one patient receiving treatment in the professional sector, William (30, male), will help to supplement and enhance the aforementioned overview of this sector. He and Lulu are this study's primary examples of professional sector patients. William would be classified as having light to moderate symptoms, whereas Lulu's case is an example of a British patient with relatively severe symptoms. For both, their medication has not had the effect they would have hoped, and they have gradually been forced to increase its potency, much like many Japanese patients who suppress their symptoms with steroids.

> [Case Study] William (30, male) 'When I was younger, the general sort of view was use steroids sparingly. Don't take oral steroids, because they will kill you.'

William and I met at a regional support group meeting of the National Eczema Society. Since we took the same train home, I asked to interview William at a later date, and he gladly accepted. The interview was conducted in a cafe, and it lasted around two hours.

On the day of the interview, William wore black cotton trousers with a grey sweater and black jacket. At the support group meeting, he had visible symptoms on his face, but they had since settled down. When asked about this, he said he had applied a large amount of topical steroids. He was cheerful and outgoing during the interview, but he told me how bullying due to his symptoms made him shy when he was younger.

William spoke of how full of stress his life was. He first developed atopic dermatitis when he was four years old. In his early years of primary school, his doctor tried to prescribe topical steroids, but after asking those around them for advice, his parents decided not to use them and instead took William to a homeopath.[3] William was then given guidance about food allergies, and he was told to avoid soy, eggs, milk, and other potential allergens. He was also given evening primrose oil, but he said that he had trouble taking it due to the smell.

In his early years of primary school, he was bullied because of his symptoms, and he had his collar bone broken twice. In secondary school, the physical abuse mostly stopped, but the verbal abuse continued, and the amount of studying he had to do increased, which led to more stress and worsening symptoms. His secondary school was a boys' school, so there was fierce competition, and he was isolated because of his symptoms. Nobody else around him had atopic dermatitis, and he was called a leper. He said the first time he had ever met another atopic dermatitis patient other than his father was at the support group meeting. Until then, he had never had anyone with whom he could discuss atopic dermatitis.

So, fact is, asthma and allergies were never even understood at all, or talked about, or aware of ten years ago, fifteen years ago, so no one really knew what eczema was. The general view, unless you have it, and you call your doctor, the general populous didn't know that, weren't aware of it, didn't understand it and didn't care… so when you were a kid, you weren't given… lessons on allergies or eczema or how to be tolerant of people or anything like that.

The people around him had no understanding of what atopic dermatitis was, so the bullying continued. It subsided when he finally became a university student and those around him were adults. He said that his four-year stint studying there was the first time he felt he fit into society. He then went on to study his master's in Edinburgh, where he was able to have fun for the first time in his life.

So it took me like four years to get around to that, and only when I moved to Edinburgh did I get better because the environment was better for me. But it was also, I was much less stressed about it… I had an awesome two years at university… I had a whole lot of friends and really enjoyed the work. There was a lot of hard work but it wasn't stressful. And I really enjoyed it.

William studied architecture, and after graduating, he moved to London, where he worked to become a qualified architect. However, the first company he worked for went bankrupt, and he joined a new company about a year before our interview. About four months before, he had stomach issues after taking antibiotics for dental treatment, and his atopic dermatitis symptoms flared up at the same time. He had used steroids regularly in the form of an inhaler since childhood to treat his asthma, but topical steroids were something he used only a little at a time.

I asked William how he felt about using steroid medication.

When I was younger, the general sort of view was use steroids sparingly. Don't take oral steroids, because they will kill you… They destroy your immune system. What was it? Mess up your thyroid, I think was one of the ones, your thyroid gland… I believe it was that and also damage one, it was your kidneys or your liver, I can't remember… That was the thought behind steroids in general, it was damaging to your body. So, any doctor you would go to see, any GP would say, yes, we will – grudgingly – will prescribe you steroids. But please use them very sparingly because you know, they could damage your liver or whatever… And I've accepted that as being what it is because everyone – every doctor you go to tells you the same thing… That is one of the things that came out of going to see the dermatologist up here. They were not so shy about steroids as everybody else was. So that's why I'm saying there seems to be a change in the thought about them. Just about the folks, the GP that I went to see who was more knowledgeable in it and these people who were in the dermatology clinic, both said you need some steroid creams, rather than don't use them.

According to William, as well as others, there is a general trend of GPs being reluctant to prescribe steroids, whereas dermatology specialists instruct patients to use them more readily. Steroid overuse in the 1960s and 1970s led to GPs and doctors who do not specialize in dermatology generally becoming wary of prescribing them. However, the protocol outlined in the current guidelines is to begin by using large doses of strong topical steroids to relieve inflammation before gradually lowering the dose and potency, and dermatologists tend to follow these guidelines as they are. William appears to have been exposed to both of these ways of thinking. I asked William how he responded when his GP told him not to use steroids while his dermatologist told him to use them.

> Even though they said it was [okay to use steroids], you've got to be careful... You take it with a pinch of salt... Basically, the advice you're given on the front of the prescription is the extreme... That's how I interpret it... It says in the front of my Betnovate, 'Use sparingly for 10 days only.' That's the extreme advice. You take it with a pinch of salt... In certain cases, okay, I can use it for longer than 10 days provided I still use it sparingly... Or you say: I use it a lot for five days, see how it is, maybe step back a little bit for a few days and then use it more for ten to five days. You interpret it... It goes back to the experimentation again... It's kind of – that's how I've done it a lot because you find that the advice you're given sometimes doesn't work. So, you know, GP says, only use moisturizers, don't use steroids... It doesn't work, you need steroids... You have to have sort of interpretation, and you've got to interpret their advice... And that's based on experience. And seeing that I've had it for all my life, that's a fair amount of experience I've had. So you tend to, you know, between your experimentation and the advice you've been given, you balance them up and you go 'Well, I'm going to completely ignore their advice and go with all what I've always had,' or like on Thursday the lady said, 'Well, why don't you try something stronger or try more steroids?' I was like, 'Okay, well what I'll do for the next couple of weeks is try more steroids and see how that goes.' And well, at the moment, it seems to be working quite well.

William thus speaks of how steroids had a negative image when he was a child, but more recently it is the accepted practice to use them more readily. It seems as though this change has impacted the way William himself has changed his view of steroids.

## Notes

1 Japan classifies topical steroid potency into five classes between one (most potent) and five (mild). Rinderon is class three (potent).
2 Dermovate is of the strongest class (most potent) of topical steroids.
3 Homoeopathy practitioners are called homoeopaths. Homoeopathy is a form of alternative medicine that involves diluting a substance that can cause the same symptoms a patient is suffering from and compressing it into a sugar pill called a remedy. By taking the remedies, patients are supposed to improve their natural healing abilities and become able to cure their ailment.

# References

Fujisawa, S. 2004, *Atopī Chiryō Kakumei (The revolution of treatment of atopic dermatitis)*, Tokyo: Nagaoka Shoten.

Fukaya, M. 1999, *Steroid Izon: Steroid wo Yametai Atopīseihifuen Kanjya no Tameni (Steroid addiction: for patients who want to stop using steroids)*, Tokyo: Tsuge Shobō Shinsha.

Fukaya, M. 2010, *Steroid Izon 2010: Nihon Hifukagakkai wa Atopīseihifuen Shinryō Guideline wo Syūsei Seyo (Steroid Addiction 2010: Alter the Guideline of Atopic Dermatitis by Japanese Dermatological Association)*, Tokyo: Iyaku Bijiransu Center.

Fukaya, M., Satō, K., Satō, M., Kimata, H., Fujisawa, S., Dozono, H., Yoshizawa, J. & Minaguchi, S. 2014, "Topical steroid addiction in atopic dermatitis", *Drug, Healthcare and Patient Safety*, vol. 6, pp. 131–138.

Furue, M., Saeki, H., Furukawa, F., Hide, M., Ohtsuki, M., Katayama, I., Sasaki, R., Sudō, H. & Takehara, K. 2009, "Atopīseihifuen shinryō guideline (Guidelines for atopic dermatitis treatment)", *Nihon Hifuka Gakkaishi (The Japanese Journal of Dermatology)*, vol. 119, no. 8, pp. 1515–1534.

Furue, M., Terao, H., Rikihisa, W., Urabe, K., Kinukawa, N., Nose, Y. & Koga, T. 2003, "Clinical dose and adverse effects of topical steroids in daily management of atopic dermatitis", *British Journal of Dermatology*, vol. 148, no. 1, pp. 128–133.

Hajar, T., Leshem, Y. A., Hanifin, J. M., Nedorost, S. T., Lio, P. A., Paller, A. S., Block, J. & Simpson, E. L. 2015, "A systematic review of topical corticosteroid withdrawal ("steroid addiction") in patients with atopic dermatitis and other dermatoses", *Journal of the American Academy of Dermatology*, vol. 72, no. 3, pp. 541–549.e2.

Hoare, C., Po, A. L. & Williams, H. U. 2000, "Systematic review of treatments for atopic eczema", *Health Technology Assessment*, vol. 4, no. 37, pp. 1–191.

Japan Allergy Tomono Kai. 2010, *Kanjya dakara Wakaru Atopīseihifuen: Soboku na Gimon kara Chiryōhō made (Atopic dermatitis, which patients can understand: from simple questions to the ways of treatment)*, Tokyo: Shōgakukan.

Katō, N., Saeki, H., Nakahara, T., Tanaka, A., Kabashima, K., Sugaya M., Murota, H., Ebihara, T., Kataoka, Y., Aihara, M. & Etō, T. 2016, "Atopīseihifuen guideline (Guidelines for atopic dermatitis treatment)", *Nihon Hifuka Gakkaishi (The Japanese Journal of Dermatology)*, vol. 126, no. 2, pp. 121–155.

National Institute for Clinical Excellence. 2004, "Frequency of application of topical corticosteroids for atopic eczema", viewed 21 March 2019, www.nice.org.uk/guidance/Ta81.

Primary Care Dermatology Society & British Association of Dermatologists. 2009, "Guidelines for the management of atopic eczema", *Skin*, vol. 39, pp. 399–402.

Rapaport, M. J. & Lebwohl, M. 2003, "Corticosteroid addiction and withdrawal in the atopic: the red burning skin syndrome", *Clinics in Dermatology*, vol. 21, no. 3, pp. 201–214.

Satō, K. 2008, *Kanjya ni Mananda Seijingata Atopy Chiryō: Datsu-steroid, Datsu-hoshitsu Ryōhō (Learning how to treat adult atopic dermatitis from patients: steroid/moisture withdrawal treatment)*, Tokyo: Tsuge Shobō Shinsha.

Scottish Intercollegiate Guidelines Network. 2011, "Management of atopic eczema in primary care: A national clinical guideline", viewed 21 March 2019, www.sign.ac.uk/assets/sign125.pdf.

Takehara, K. 2000, *Atopī Business (The atopy business)*, Tokyo: Bungeishunjyū.

Takeuchi, K. & Takenoshita, T. 2009, *Kōhei, Muryō, Kokuei wo Tsuranuku Eikoku no Iryō Kaikaku (Fair, free, and state-run, the UK medical reform)*, Tokyo: Shūeisha.

Tamaki, A. 2008, *Ninin Sankyaku de Naosu Atopy: Chiryō no Saizensen kara (Curing atopy with cooperation: from the frontier of treatment)*, Osaka: Seifūdō Shoten.

Yamamoto, S. & Kawano, Y. 2006, *Atopīseihifuen Shinryō Guideline 2006 (Guidelines for atopic dermatitis treatment 2006)*, Tokyo: Kyōwa Kikaku.

# 4    The folk sector

## Alternative medicine

### Alternative medicine in Japan

In both Japan and the UK, health care comes in many diverse forms, including herbal medicine and homeopathy. All the forms outside of modern medicine fall within the folk sector, and they will be referred to here as *alternative medicine*. Alternative medicine has been a significant form of health care, and this is certainly the case with atopic dermatitis treatment in Japan.

Japan saw such an upsurge in alternative medicine related to atopic dermatitis in the 1990s that it spawned the term *Atopy Business*. These alternative treatments varied widely in type, efficacy, and safety, and some even made use of topical steroids while fraudulently denying this. The folk sector in Japan, as becomes immediately apparent, is simply not structured in a way that guarantees a high quality of treatment. Takuya Tsujiuchi points out that the level of pluralism and diversity evident in complementary and alternative medicine (CAM) in Japan could be called profusive or rhizomatic. It lacks much of the systematic, integrated, hierarchical structure of modern medicine and remains largely unregulated. However, in 1998, the Japanese Association for Alternative, Complementary and Traditional Medicine (JACT) was established with Kazuhiko Atsumi at its centre, and in 2000, Atsumi went on to found the Japanese Society for Integrative Medicine (JIM). Tsujiuchi (2004) saw this as an attempt by Japanese complementary and alternative medicine to begin to standardize and form its own hierarchical structure, but they have not yet had much success. Although alternative medicine in Japan has started attempting to regulate itself somewhat through formal associations, a cursory look at alternative treatments for atopic dermatitis shows little evidence of actual regulation. Patients can do little more than apply trial and error in selecting treatments from the disordered jumble of those available and then testing out on themselves the ones they think may suit them.

Dermatologist Kazuhiko Takehara carried out a study into 'inappropriate treatments' for atopic dermatitis between 1998 and 1999, investigating the types of treatments patients were using then. According to his findings, the vast majority, 162 of the 191 patients who participated (84.8%), had tried a specific form of alternative treatment (Takehara, 2000). My own findings (Table 4.1) from my interviews, during which I asked what treatments patients had previously received,[1] also bear this out. The overwhelming majority of the patients I interviewed have tried some form of alternative medicine at some point. Table 4.1 also includes important information about patients' histories with standard treatment.

*Table 4.1* An overview of the treatments interview participants had tried (Japan)

| | Pseudonym | Sex | Age | Steroid use | Treatments |
|---|---|---|---|---|---|
| 1 | Michiaki | M | 21 | [a] | Lush brand soaps, Protopic ointment |
| 2 | Wataru | M | 30 | [a] | Oigami Hot Spring, Toyotomi Hot Spring, soaps, moisturizer, body work, 3 in 1 stress-release programme, supplements, Bach flower remedies, pillows, SOD-rich foods, chlorine-removing shower head, drinking water, coaching, finger pressure, sleeping medicine, using vitamin C to remove chlorine from bath water, special diets |
| 3 | Asami | F | 31 | [a] | Hydropathic treatment, supplements, capsulated enzyme, wave therapy |
| 4 | Kanae | F | 32 | [a] | Herbal medicine, vegetarian diet, perilla juice, applying salt on skin |
| 5 | Yōsuke | M | 33 | [a] | Special diets, macrobiotics, bath additives |
| 6 | Ryōhei | M | 34 | [a] | Body work, gluten-free diet, bath additives |
| 7 | Satomi | F | 36 | [a] | No answer |
| 8 | Yoshimi | F | 40 | [a] | Linseed oil, biotin, hythiol, lactobacillus |
| 9 | Satoru | M | 38 | [a] | Shoulder massage at aesthetic plastic surgery clinic |
| 10 | Junya | M | 39 | [a] | Japan Ombas brand hot spring water remedy, soaps, allergen avoidance, chlorine-removing shower head |
| 11 | Yukie | F | 39 | [a] | Chlorella, hypo-sensitization therapy, aloe vera juice, pyroligneous acid and bamboo vinegar lotion, hydropathic treatment, anti-tick bed, spiritual mediums, supplements, macrobiotics, yoga |
| 12 | Kimiko | F | 41 | [a] | No answer |
| 13 | Saki | F | 46 | [a] | Pine tar ointment, moisturizer, Protopic ointment, fasting, herbal medicine, water filter, organic vegetables, 100% cotton clothes, chlorine-removing shower head, Dyson brand vacuum cleaner |

| | Pseudonym | Sex | Age | Steroid use | Treatments |
|---|---|---|---|---|---|
| 14 | Ryūhei | M | 49 | a | Japan Ombas brand hot spring water remedy, acupuncture, massage, fasting |
| 15 | Kōsuke | M | 24 | b | Herbal medicine |
| 16 | Natsuko | F | 24 | b | No answer |
| 17 | Akio | M | 30 | b | *Aojiru* (green juice) nutritional supplement, herbal medicine, chlorine-removing shower head, hot spring water remedy, restricted diets, hospitalization, chitin and chitosan |
| 18 | Shinobu | F | 31 | b | No answer |
| 19 | Sae | F | 34 | b | Acidic water |
| 20 | Jin | M | 35 | b | Thalassotherapy, herbal medicine, horse oil, squalene, shark oil, baby oil, ointment, supplements, *aojiru* (green juice), SOD-rich foods |
| 21 | Kiyoka | F | 41 | b | Herbal medicine, lactobacillus, hot spring water remedy, face-washing with acidic water, samemilon (shark oil), Qigong, ionized calcium drink, Amway brand cosmetics, organic vegetables, avoiding fast food and convenience-store food |
| 22 | Michie | F | 22 | c | Niwa Naturopathic Treatment at Tosashimizu Hospital |
| 23 | Miyako | F | 22 | c | Horse oil, herbal medicine, sweet tea, wet tea packs, acupuncture tapping therapy, cupping therapy, soaps, olive oil |
| 24 | Kōji | M | 25 | c | Steroids |
| 25 | Ayami | F | 25 | c | Acupuncture, Thermie therapy, light treatment, acupressure, hot spring mineral water, soaps |
| 26 | Yoshiki | M | 26 | c | No answer |
| 27 | Shiori | F | 27 | c | Entering pool and sea water with cling film around her body |
| 28 | Sakie | F | 29 | c | Steroids, ciclosporin |
| 29 | Kōichi | M | 35 | c | Steroids, herbal medicine, chlorella |
| 30 | Shukuko | F | No answer | c | No answer |

a  People who had stopped using topical steroids.
b  Those who had stopped using steroids in the past but had resumed use by the time of the interview.
c  Those who had continuously used steroids.

As shown in the table, the forms of alternative medicine used by patients are incredibly diverse. They include treatments related to food, such as macrobiotics, organic vegetables, aloe vera juice, chlorella, *aojiru* (green juice), and restricted diets; treatments related to water, such as hot springs, seawater, acidic water, and chlorine removal; diverse forms of treatment, such as herbal medicine, acupuncture, acupressure, the Thermie therapy, and phototherapy; treatments applied to the skin, such as horse oil, squalene, baby oil, pine tar ointment, and soaps; treatments relatively well-known in the atopic dermatitis space, such as Niwa Naturopathic Treatment at Tosashimizu Hospital (based on SOD-rich foods) and Japan Ombas; and even spiritual mediums. As this level of diversity makes clear, the market for alternative medicine is huge and has shown a remarkable level of expansion.

Each form of alternative medicine has its own explanatory model and treatment goals, so it is difficult to make generalizations about alternative medicine as a whole. Nevertheless, it is possible to find some general trends and common factors among the various treatments. As Ikeda (1995) points out, alternative medicine is typically not something completely removed from modern medicine, but is instead influenced by it in some way. For example, this could be in the complementary sense that alternative medicine provides things that modern medicine fails to, such as lengthy consultation times or more compassionate care, or in the sense that alternative medicine attracts patients who reject modern medicine.

Based on patient case studies from the literature and research currently available on the appeal and characteristics of alternative medicine, these seem to be their six most significant shared characteristics:

1  Alternative medicine is not associated with harmful side effects.

   Sarah Cant and Ursula Sharma (1999), who carried out research on British complementary and alternative medicine, and John Zwicky and American Medical Association (1993), which carried out research on American alternative medicine, conclude that one of the reasons alternative medicine attracts patients is the belief that it employs naturalistic treatments that do not have harmful side effects. Although this might be nothing more than a misperception, the image of safety does nevertheless offer people peace of mind and attracts them to alternative medicine.

   The idea of a lack of side effects attracting patients is of particular significance regarding atopic dermatitis. A large number of the people who turn to alternative medicine are driven by a fear of steroids' side effects, and since they believe they can avoid using steroids this way, they try out these purportedly safer treatments.

2  Alternative medicine offers hope.

   Catherine Zollman and Andrew Vickers (1999) point to hope as a key part of the appeal of alternative medicine. The majority of the people trying out these treatments have already been under the care of modern medicine, and they have finally turned to alternative medicine for a cure after trying everything else. Alternative medicine is able to provide these patients with the hope of a cure.

   Together with the perception of a lack of side effects, the hope of a cure for atopic dermatitis is also a major factor in attracting these patients to alternative medicine. Since patients are unable to cure their atopic dermatitis through standard treatment, they are forced to look for hope elsewhere. For patients who are feeling the limitations of standard treatment in particular, alternative medicine shines as the last beacon of hope for curing their atopic dermatitis.

The fact that alternative medicine offers patients hope is in contrast to modern medicine's stance of denying patients unfounded hope. It is well known that the placebo effect is significant—that dosing patients with fake medicine that these patients believe is real can bring about an actual recovery. In fact, it is precisely to eliminate the possibility of this placebo effect that modern medicine carries out double-blind trials to measure the efficacy of medication. A double-blind trial involves splitting participants into two groups: one group that receives the drug being tested and one control group that receives a placebo. The efficacy of the drug is measured without either the participants or the doctors involved being aware of which group is which. In this way, the pharmaceutical drugs can be shown to exert their intended effects regardless of the participants' state of mind.

Conversely, within alternative medicine, the state of mind of the patient is seen as a significant factor in influencing the efficacy of the treatment. By believing that they are healing, patients find peace of mind, and their natural ability to heal is enhanced. This can then lead to a full recovery, as numerous cases of trial participants show. In other words, it could be said that by convincing patients they will heal, alternative medicine proactively harnesses the placebo effect. For these reasons, forms of alternative medicine can be seen as providing patients with a potentially positive hope, but there is also the risk of the level of hope rising so high that patients become all the more dejected if the treatment fails (Zollman and Vickers, 1999).

3   Patients can actively select and participate in treatment themselves.

Zollman and Vickers (1999), Cant and Sharma (1999), and Zwicky and American Medical Association (1993) all claim that part of the appeal of alternative medicine is in the way it allows patients to actively select and participate in treatment themselves. Cant and Sharma (1999) especially emphasize the sense of control patients gain by being able to choose their own treatment.

In the case of atopic dermatitis, symptoms worsen and improve for unknown reasons, so patients have very little sense of control. In particular, patients who stop using steroids see a rapid decline in their condition at first, which further reduces any sense of control, and sometimes leads to them feeling helpless and overwhelmed. At this point, it is difficult for them to sit by in silence as their condition worsens, and they are eager to attempt anything they can in order to gain even the slightest relief from their symptoms. Since alternative medicine generally involves patients choosing from a wide range of treatments themselves, it is necessary for them to take a more active role, rather than simply receiving prescriptions from their doctors. In this way, patients feel as though they are contributing to their own recovery, and this becomes part of the appeal of alternative medicine.

4    There is intimate communication with the healer.

The intimate level of communication shared between healers and patients, including some level of bodily contact, can also be counted as an appeal of alternative medicine (Cant and Sharma, 1999; Zollman and Vickers, 1999; Muraoka, 2000). The lengthy consultation times seen in alternative medicine influence this greater sense of connection. Conversely, consultation times are so short within modern medicine that they are often ridiculed in Japan as 'three-minute treatment,' which leaves little opportunity for doctors and patients to communicate closely. The atopic dermatitis patients interviewed as part of this book spoke of simply being prescribed steroids each time they attended a clinic, with a bare minimum of communication with their doctor. In comparison, there was a close level of communication with several forms of alternative medicine.

5    A convincing explanatory model is presented.

According to Zwicky and American Medical Association (1993), the language used within alternative medicine is relatively simple, and alternative medicine appeals to patients with its easy-to-understand and persuasive explanatory model.

The process of recovery during steroid withdrawal treatments follows a typical narrative, and this is one of the factors that makes it convincing for patients. Many cases of steroid withdrawal treatment can be thought of as progressing through the following stages: (1) steroid medication is discontinued, (2) a relapse occurs and symptoms are exacerbated, and (3) the atopic dermatitis is cured. This persuasive narrative structure has a great deal in common with a rite of passage, which Arnold van Gennep (2004) described as having three stages: separation, liminality, and incorporation.

1    Separation: Moving away from a state in which steroids were routinely used.
2    Liminality: During the relapse period, there are frequent absences from school or work, and a general withdrawal from society.
3    Incorporation: Recovery leads to a return to normal life.

From the interviews, it becomes apparent that there are patients who never see an improvement in their symptoms after stopping steroids and those who experience a relapse even if they do see an initial improvement. The three-stage narrative of steroid withdrawal treatment, which promises that one's atopic dermatitis will heal as long as one can get over the liminal stage of the relapse, is structured in a way that is very easy to understand, but there are many cases that do not actually conform to this narrative. The easy-to-follow narrative and explanatory model nonetheless have the power to convince patients of success, making them believe they need only get through a relapse of indeterminate length in order to heal, and this draws them to alternative medicine.

6    Large amounts of advertising, publicity, and information in the media.

Especially in the sphere of mental illnesses, it has been argued that the media play a significant role in how diseases are constructed. This idea has been discussed as the problem of 'disease mongering,' which refers to how pharmaceutical companies use the media to make healthy people believe that they are ill so that these companies can expand the consumer base for their products (Moynihan et al., 2002). Regarding this point about the media's key role in touting diseases, the situation of the Japanese alternative medicine market shows many parallels to this phenomenon.

Although this is not the case in the UK, information regarding alternative medicine is abundant in all forms of media in Japan, including television, radio, magazines, newspapers, the Internet, and books, and this could be one of the factors behind the success of alternative medicine in Japan. There are a large number of programmes related to health on Japanese television, including *Tameshite Gatten* (NHK General TV), *Omoikkiri TV* (NTV), and *Karada no Kimochi* (TBS). The impressive influence these programmes have on people can be seen when food products are introduced on the programmes that quickly sell out everywhere the following day. There are also a large number of magazines on the topic of health, including *Sōkai* (Makino Publishing), *Hatsuratsu Genki* (Geibunsha), *Wakasa* (Wakasa Publishing), and *Yuhobika* (Makino Publishing).

There are various regulations that supposedly place limitations on alternative medicine advertising, including the Pharmaceutical Affairs Act, which states that 'any pharmaceutical product that has not received the approval of the Minister of Health, Labour and Welfare cannot advertise regarding the name, manufacturing process, efficacy or performance of that product,' and the Health Promotion Act, which states that 'false or misleading advertising regarding health-related effects is prohibited.' Nevertheless, exploiting something of a legal grey zone, alternative medicine advertising can be seen across all mediums, including television, magazines, newspapers, and the Internet.

As an example, there is a method known in Japan as the bible scheme. Since advertising the efficacy or effectiveness of a product directly would run afoul of the Pharmaceutical Affairs Act, the tactic is to release a book detailing these claims, including the sales information at the end, and thereby allowing customers to purchase the products. Releasing the information in the form of a book means that it is protected in the name of freedom of expression, and thus the method is able to circumvent advertising regulations. It also provides a strategy for advertising the product in the media, since the book itself can be advertised legally in newspapers.

Listing the efficacy or effectiveness of unapproved drugs in the form of a catalogue is also in breach of the Pharmaceutical Affairs Act. However, there are cases of unapproved drugs being advertised in magazines that are very similar to catalogues, since it is legal to list such things in a magazine.

The even more lax regulations on the Internet mean that false and misleading advertising is rife. In 2010, the Consumer Affairs Agency of Japan toughened its stance, announcing a new policy of publicly naming businesses guilty of misleading advertising if they did not improve after receiving a warning. However, the amount of alternative medicine advertising and information circulated by the media is vast, and it remains to be seen if government regulations will have any effect.

As will be discussed, there is comparatively less false or misleading advertising in the UK. The relative trend of tolerance towards alternative medicine advertising in Japan could be seen as one of the reasons that alternative medicine targeting atopic dermatitis in Japan has prospered to the extent that it has.

[Case Study] Asami (28, female): 'I never thought about giving up on everything. I wanted to cure it so bad.'

Asami's case is illustrative of a patient's experience of using alternative medicine. Since Asami's way of thinking has been strongly influenced by alternative medicine, an explanatory model characteristic of alternative medicine arises in her story.

Asami has attempted steroid withdrawal twice. She first tried it when she was in the third grade of high school, and on this occasion her condition stabilized and she was able to remain symptomless for five years without any use of steroids. She was 24 the second time she tried it, and this withdrawal led to a much worse flare-up than the first. She ended up trying several forms of alternative medicine to deal with this flare-up. Within alternative medicine, treatment is often seen as 'a new transcendental state' (Fuller, 1989), which is a special kind of state like having been reborn, and Asami's view largely aligns with this idea. Although Asami experienced something of a lull after getting through her rebound, she described the feeling of recovering from her symptoms this way in her interview:

> Maybe this is a bit of an exaggeration, but it kind of felt like being born again. Like I'd returned to my old self. I've seen people who've truly been cured, though, and I think that's when you can really say you've been born again. I have a friend who said she really started her life over again from that point.

After her second attempt at steroid withdrawal at 24, Asami tried various forms of alternative medicine, including live-in treatment, moxibustion, hydrotherapy, wave therapy, and supplements. She explains how she felt some effects from each treatment at first, but her symptoms would return after some time. However, even if her symptoms did worsen, Asami did not quit the treatment straightaway, but would instead attempt to bear through it for a while. Such an attitude to accept and bear a flare-up of symptoms could be seen as a unique and deeply rooted feature of alternative medicine treatment. Within several forms of alternative medicine when symptoms flare up after discontinuing steroids, it is explained to the patient that it is because of the release of steroid toxins that have accumulated in the body, and patients are thus assured that persevering can cure atopic dermatitis. As a result, continuing symptoms are seen as proof that steroids still remain in the body and that a cure cannot be achieved until they are completely expelled. This explanation allowed Asami to frame her symptoms in a positive way, and this was the foundation of her attitude towards continuing treatment.

The wave therapy Asami received also seemed to be based on an explanatory model particular to alternative medicine. When asked exactly what wave therapy was, Asami attempted to explain:

ASAMI: It's kind of like Qigong. You take the waves into your body, and it's true with Qigong too, but the relapse is really bad. … It doesn't happen for regular people, but if you have steroids inside you because of atopic dermatitis, then it happens. I'm scared to do it too. You sweat, more and more. I was clutching at straws to get better at that point, since I was trying anything. … But when you can't sleep at night for seven or eight years, you just don't have any energy. The fatigue builds up when you're receiving treatment for so long. The stress, too, or at least the will to carry on is sucked out of you.

AUTHOR: Didn't you think of changing treatments when it got bad?

ASAMI: Well, I thought I'd get better if I got all of the bad stuff out. There were times when I didn't believe it, but there were times when I just wanted it all out. Even if my symptoms were okay, when I thought about getting married and having kids, I wanted the steroids out of me. I wanted something to be happy about. So, the steroids were coming out from the inside little by little each day. Healing was my goal.

As Asami explains, the thinking behind this wave therapy is that the more you endure the flare-up in symptoms, the more steroids are released from your body, bringing you closer to a cure. They see steroids as providing temporary relief from symptoms, while at the same time pushing patients further away from a cure. The reason patients endure such terrible symptoms is their desire to cure their condition no matter what it takes, and this becomes the motivation that supports them through the painful treatment.

> I definitely thought I could cure myself, and there were times when maybe I thought it wouldn't happen, just for me, but basically, I thought it would happen. No matter what treatment I was trying, I felt reassured when I saw other people doing it, and I really felt motivation to do it. I thought I had to. I just had to.

While Asami harbours doubts about whether or not she can attain a cure, what can be felt from the way she speaks is a desire to believe in a cure, a desire so strong that it erases these doubts. When asked if she had ever had symptoms that had pushed her over the edge and made her want to give up all forms of treatment, she responded as follows:

> I was always doing something. I never thought about giving everything up. I wanted to get better so badly. I think people like me need something to believe in when we're at our worst.

As Asami says, when her symptoms were at their worst, she searched for something to believe in (i.e., a curative treatment), and this is a commonly shared attitude among many patients. It could also be said that several forms of alternative medicine aimed at atopic dermatitis patients exploit this mentality. While their desire to quit using steroids and cure atopic dermatitis provides them encouragement and support, it can also lead to denial; patients might refuse to admit their lack of improvement and their pouring excessive amounts of time and money into treatment. The hope of healing offered by alternative medicine is thus a double-edged sword, and the line between the right and wrong of treatments that purport to heal is constantly blurred.

## Alternative medicine in the UK

### *Differences between alternative medicine in Japan and the UK*

As alluded to in the previous section, the folk sector (i.e., alternative medicine) in the UK is more constrained in many ways than in Japan. The biggest difference specifically regarding alternative medicine for atopic dermatitis in the UK and Japan is that the term or concept of *steroid withdrawal treatment* simply does not exist in the UK. However, the lack of steroid withdrawal treatment does not necessarily mean patients think positively of steroids. A study conducted in Nottingham reported that 72.5% of patients had concerns about using topical steroids, and 24% of patients had shown non-compliance with steroid treatment in the past (Charman et al., 2000). A strong sense of wariness towards topical steroids was also apparent in my interviews in the UK. Despite this cautionary attitude towards topical steroids, however, the idea that stopping topical steroids could actually cure atopic dermatitis is not something people subscribe to in the UK. In Japan, on the other hand, as already discussed, this idea has gained popularity among both steroid withdrawal doctors and alternative medicine practitioners. These health care providers in Japan have witnessed cases of patients giving up steroids and having their symptoms improve, and it was from these observations that the idea of discontinuing steroids as a cure for atopic dermatitis was conceived. Particularly within the alternative medicine industry, claims that stopping steroid use will cure patients' atopic dermatitis offer hope to patients who are already against steroids, and these claims draw them towards this industry's alternative treatment plans. Promoting this way of thinking thus seems very good for business.

In the UK, as the case study of Haley will show, there are also people who stop using steroids. However, in this case, the thinking is not that atopic dermatitis is cured by discontinuing steroids, but, more modestly, that discontinuing steroids is acceptable if atopic dermatitis symptoms disappear. This runs directly counter to the way steroid withdrawal treatment frames the process. Treatments that force patients to endure severe relapses to cure atopic dermatitis do not exist in the UK. Instead, forms of treatment with some amount of credibility are typically used, including homeopathy, Chinese herbal medicine, and acupuncture.

*Table 4.2* An overview of the treatments interview participants had tried (UK)

| | Pseudonym | Sex | Age | Steroid use | Treatments |
|---|---|---|---|---|---|
| 1 | Annick (unknown nationality) | F | 26 | a | Chinese herbal medicine, steroids, water-soluble cream |
| 2 | Allie (Australian) | F | 28 | a | Acupuncture, echinacea purpurea cream, calamine lotion, homeopathy |
| 3 | Penn (Polish) | M | 32 | a | Antihistamines, allantoin cream, Neutrogena brand moisturizer, vitamin supplements, allergy-friendly diets, cream, Aveeno brand moisturizer, vitamin A cream, cholesterol cream |
| 4 | Hayley (British) | F | 52 | a | Yoga, meditation, psychological therapy, acupuncture, Chinese herbal medicine, homeopathy |
| 5 | Anne (Filipino) | F | 29 | b | Chinese herbal medicine, vegetarian diet, avoidance of gym exercise, supplements of sunflower oil and vitamins, steroids, moisturizing cream |
| 6 | Jeff (British) | M | 28 | c | Homeopathy, moisturizing cream |
| 7 | William (British) | M | 30 | c | Homeopathy, 'wet wrap' bandages, evening primrose oil |
| 8 | Frank (British) | M | 30 | c | Steroids |
| 9 | James (Bangladeshi) | M | 32 | c | Chinese herbal medicine, acupuncture, allergy testing, homeopathy |
| 10 | Benjamin(British) | M | 46 | c | Homeopathy, hypnotherapy, avoidance of citrus, acupuncture, antihistamines, steroids |
| 11 | Lulu (British) | F | 47 | c | Herbal remedy, homeopathy, Chinese herbal medicine |
| 12 | Shelly (British) | F | 65 | c | Steroids, E45 brand bath oil, antibiotics |

a  People who had stopped using topical steroids.
b  Those who had stopped using steroids in the past but had resumed use by the time of the interview.
c  Those who had continuously used steroids.

Table 4.2 summarizes the treatments used in the past by the interview participants in the UK. Excluding treatments based on modern medicine, including antihistamines, antibiotics, products by E45 (a company specializing in skin care), and 'wet wrap' bandages, the main alternative treatments used were homeopathy (seven people), Chinese herbal medicine (five people), and acupuncture (four people). Homeopathy is not common in Japan, but it is a highly popular form of treatment in the UK, and it has even been available on the NHS since its founding. Kate Thomas et al.'s (1995) report on the most used forms of CAM in the UK lists the top three in order, as acupuncture, homeopathy, and osteopathy,[2] which gives some insight into the popularity of homeopathy. Whereas patients in Japan try a widely varying range of alternative treatments, it could be said that alternative medicine in the UK comprises treatments that have attained at least some form of credibility.

### Advertising regulations

It is difficult to determine exactly why steroid withdrawal treatment does not exist in the UK, but an explanation of UK advertising regulations can provide some insight into why such treatments are not commonly known there. As mentioned previously, alternative medicine and advertising in Japan circulates through all forms of media, including the Internet, magazines, books, and newspapers. Although laws prohibiting false and misleading advertising exist, such as the Pharmaceutical Affairs Act and Health Promotion Act, various forms of such advertising still seem to slip through loopholes. Many alternative medicine advertisements attract clients by claiming to be able to cure atopic dermatitis, but since there is no known existing cure for atopic dermatitis, any claim to provide one constitutes false or misleading advertising. Operating in an environment that permits the proliferation of such advertising seems to have enabled alternative medicine in Japan to acquire clients and secure the level of growth it has.

The UK is known for having some of the strictest advertising regulations in the world, and it is extremely rare to see the kind of false or misleading advertising that is prevalent in Japan. Behind these regulations in the UK, there is a history of a great struggle involving the advertising industry, the government, and consumers, which continued throughout the 20th century. At the start of the 20th century, it was common to see false or misleading advertising. According to Masaharu Arai's (1994) research on British advertising, the efficacy statements of branded drugs in a 1934 report submitted to a government committee by the Royal College of Surgeons of England were 'always exaggerated, and generally fraudulent,' and some of the drugs had absolutely none of the purported effects.

Investigating British newspaper advertising from the end of the 19th century to the beginning of the 20th century shows that there were actually even misleading advertisements precisely for atopic dermatitis treatments. For example, the 9 April 1904 edition of the *Essex Newsman* contained the following advertisement.

> ECZEMA – The World's Greatest Skin Humour. Affects Every Age and Condition. The Only Sure Cure is Cuticura.
>
> The Cuticura treatment is at once agreeable, speedy, economical and comprehensive. Bathe the affected parts freely with hot water and Cuticura Soap, to cleanse the surface of crusts and scales, and soften the thickened cuticle. Dry, without hard rubbing, and apply Cuticura Ointment to allay itching, irritation and inflammation, and soothe and heal, and, lastly, take Cuticura Resolvent, or Pills, to cool and cleanse the blood. This treatment affords instant relief, permits rest and sleep in the severest forms of eczema and other itching, burning and scaly humours, and points to a speedy, permanent and economical cure of torturing, disfiguring humours, eczemas,

rashes and inflammations, from infancy to age, when all other remedies and the best physicians fail.

(Potter Drug and Chemistry Corporation 1904; 3)

It is clear that, at the very least, advertisements for products claiming to provide cures existed in the UK from the end of the 19th century to the start of the 20th century. Various kinds of advertising regulations thus had to be introduced to achieve the current state of advertising.

In the first half of the 20th century, misleading advertisements for wonder drugs for rash-like conditions, as well as diseases like cancer and tuberculosis, were so common that they prompted the Cancer Act 1939, banning advertisements for cancer miracle drugs, and the Pharmacy & Medicines Act 1941, prohibiting advertisements for remedies for tuberculosis and other diseases. In addition to legislation like this limiting the advertising of branded drugs, pharmaceutical manufacturers collectively created self-imposed advertising regulations. This was a calculated attempt to ward off further legislation. For example, in 1919, pharmaceutical manufacturers formed the Proprietary Association of Great Britain, and established a system of self-regulation, including regulations for advertising, to which they jointly agreed to adhere. This developed into the more substantial British Code of Standards relating to the Advertising of Medicines and Treatments in 1948, and all drug-related advertising came to be regulated in accordance with this (Arai, 1994).

The legislation and regulations proved effective in the UK, and it became very difficult to produce advertisements claiming to cure atopic dermatitis like those found in Japan. With such strict advertising regulations, forms of alternative medicine claiming cures that they cannot actually provide have no doubt been suppressed. The fact that nothing like the Japanese Atopy Business exists in the UK could therefore be attributed to the influence that these strict advertising regulations have had.

[Case Study] Alternative medicine practitioner Terry

While I was living in the UK in 2010, an introduction through an acquaintance offered me the opportunity to interview Terry (pseudonym), an alternative medicine practitioner. This gave me the opportunity to gain a better understanding of what alternative medicine in the UK is like. I interviewed Terry at the clinic in which he practised, on a nice street along the River Thames, next to a pet shop and a comic shop. The clinic's sign listed the services acupuncture, chiropractic, homeopathy, massage, and counselling. The clinic had a white exterior, and the inside was pristine with clean wooden flooring and neatly displayed jars of what appeared to be herbal medicine. When I entered the clinic, a young woman at the reception called for Terry.

A tall man in an earth-toned plaid shirt, Terry looked friendly and easy-going with black, slightly scruffy hair, big eyes, and some stubble over his fair skin. He was 43 years old and said that he had been working in London for 12 years. He gave off the impression of being a kind person with an underlying sensitivity.

We spoke in Terry's consultation room in the basement. This room had no door and felt very open. It was furnished with a single bed, and the large desk that Terry used abutted the wall. There were two chairs, one for Terry and one for his patient. A model of the human skeleton was placed beside the bed, and vials of homeopathic medicine were scattered across the desk. The room had a cozy, relaxed atmosphere.

Terry was responsible for homeopathy, the Alexander technique, and Western and Chinese herbal remedies. He generally used homeopathy to treat atopic dermatitis, and he prepared remedies specific to patients' needs. According to him, it takes time for the skin to recover, but symptoms generally die down after two to three weeks, and continue improving over the following months. When I asked him what percentage of patients found homeopathy effective, Terry considered this a few moments before estimating it to be somewhere below 50%.

I asked Terry for a basic outline of the philosophy behind homeopathy. He explained that in homeopathy, the skin is seen as a single organ, and by strengthening other organs, such as the liver, kidneys, and lungs, the burden on the skin is reduced. However, since homeopathy works through energy, or 'life-force,' it cannot be explained scientifically. In other words, biomedicine affects the visible organs of the body, but homeopathy acts on functions of the body which cannot be perceived. Terry told me that although medical treatment carried out by the NHS is effective for serious accidents or diseases that leave people close to death, and he does often recommend such treatment, it does not provide suitable care for people closer to health. According to Terry, the alternative medicine that he and his colleagues practise is able to fill this void.

When I asked him about topical steroids and whether he sometimes prescribes them, Terry said that he was not able to prescribe them since he did not have the necessary license, but that he did prescribe calendula (marigold) cream. This treatment can be used alongside topical steroids, and the aim is to reduce the dose of steroids gradually over time. The majority of these patients are children, and there are cases when topical steroids can be discontinued completely. Ascertaining the cause behind flare-ups is difficult, so Terry has to listen carefully and objectively to his patients to help him search for potential causes.

In fact, Terry had severe rashes on his hands when he was around ten years old, and he had used topical steroids for treatment. After trying homeopathy when a friend introduced it to him, he said he shed his skin almost like a snake after two to three weeks. Underneath was a layer of new and pristine skin, and he recovered completely. He said this personal healing experience is what led him to becoming a homeopath himself. He injured his back at age 25 and found it hard to continue his job. He wanted to choose a job that would allow him to manage his back pain, and since it would not bind him to an office for long periods, he began aiming to be a homeopathy practitioner. When I remarked on his level of personal experience, he responded that everyone in the alternative medicine industry is in it because of personal experience.

Finally, I asked Terry what kinds of questions he asks patients at the clinic. He said that during the initial consultation, which typically lasts an hour, he asks a diverse range of questions on various topics, including current symptoms, eating habits, the time of onset, medical history, and family history.

From Terry's interview, it became apparent that, in both Japan and the UK, alternative medicine has a number of relatively consistent factors. As discussed, alternative medicine has generated demand by providing what modern medicine fails to. Terry further illustrated the complementary role it can have, showing that it is able to provide things like longer consultation times and alternative explanatory models, for example, the holistic philosophy in which strengthening multiple organs relieves the burden on the skin or the idea of exploiting imperceptible bodily functions.

Haley's experience as a patient who received alternative treatment and was eventually able to discontinue topical steroids provides another important perspective on the folk sector's appeal.

[Case Study] Haley (52, female) 'So I know it's not my skin. It must be what I'm eating.'

When I was searching for atopic dermatitis patients to interview, a friend helpfully introduced me to her grandmother, Haley. I interviewed Haley at her home in Newbury. Haley greeted me warmly with a hug, relieved to finally find me at Newbury station. Haley was slim and cheerful and looked as though she was in her late 40s. Her red hair reached below her shoulders, and she spoke clearly with a smile that never left her face. As she drove me back to her house in her vivid blue Nissan, she talked about her granddaughter.

Haley's house had two storeys and a garden. Guests were first greeted by a flower bed filled with a mixture of pink and yellow tulips as well as other white and blue flowers. After going through the wooden gate, a lovely green garden filled the thirty-some square metres in front of the house. A large maple tree overflowing with green leaves towered above it all, and light pink clematis were in full bloom. Through the front door and to the right was a side entrance to the house, where Haley's husband sat in a chair enjoying the sunlight. He offered a simple greeting. He looked to be in his 50s, with a face that was somehow captivating. His smile suited the cheerful impression he gave, but as a man of few words, he spoke in his husky voice only infrequently.

We sat in the living room for our interview, basking in the sunlight from the garden. The home had a spacious, open design that merged the living room, dining room, and a PC corner into one. Three European-style landscapes painted in acrylic adorned the walls. I later learnt that Haley had painted them herself. Before the red sofa were the television and a radiator. Mountings along the wall were decorated with deep purple gemstones and a lamp made from a pink stone.

Haley's first outbreak of atopic dermatitis was six months after she was born. She believes her outbreak was due to her mother foregoing breastfeeding for formula on her doctor's advice. She has two older brothers. One was breastfed for seven months and has never suffered any atopic dermatitis symptoms. The other was breastfed for only three months, when Haley's mother could no longer lactate, and he later developed asthma, atopic dermatitis, and hay fever after being fed artificial baby milk as a replacement. Haley used topical steroids every time her symptoms flared up; her condition throughout childhood was constantly 'extremely severe.' Her doctor told her the symptoms would go away when she grew up, but she never saw any improvement. Her entire face remained red, swollen, and itchy.

When Haley was in university, she read an article that suggested atopic dermatitis patients should avoid milk, wheat, and eggs.

> When I left home and I started looking after myself, I thought, 'Right, what can I do?' So, I saw this article and it gave me some hope that I might be able to do something.

Since her condition was so severe, Haley decided to give this a try, and stopped consuming milk, wheat, and eggs. As a result, the symptoms on her legs improved very slightly. Although the results were minimal, when she ate eggs again after three months, her throat felt prickly, and she realized that she might be allergic to eggs. At the time, in the 1960s, any connection between atopic dermatitis and food was unknown, and she was not given any advice relating to her diet, so she continued consuming allergens until she was 21. Sometime after this, while still in university, her doctor told her that zinc could be effective for atopic dermatitis and prescribed her some supplements. Her symptoms improved greatly after trying it.

Soon after graduating from university, at age 23, Haley married her husband. At the time, she was not eating milk or eggs, but since it was difficult to get by without bread, she continued eating wheat. Since there was not yet any gluten-free flour, soy products, or milk substitutes, it must have taken a significant amount of effort to maintain such a diet without allergens.

When she was around 26 or 27, Haley began to see a Chinese herbal medicine practitioner. She was instructed to boil herbs to take every day, and at the same time avoid consuming milk and wheat. When she stopped eating wheat, the once rough skin on her legs softened. She also went to see a naturopath, as well as trying the caveman diet. The caveman diet is also called the Paleolithic diet or hunter-gatherer diet, and it involves avoiding foods such as dairy products, refined salt, sugar, and oils. After trying this for a few weeks, Haley saw a moderate improvement in her symptoms, but they flared up again soon after. She did not have much money back then, and she believes not being able to afford enough zinc was one of the reasons behind her flare-ups. The particular diet she was following also involved eating a large amount of the same type of food at once, and then doing the same with a different food; for example, she would eat a great deal of sesame for a few days and then a lot of shrimp for a few days. She says this made her more sensitive to the allergens she had consumed.

Haley later read a book by American mystic Edgar Cayce, which left a deep impression on her. It is said that Cayce possessed special powers that allowed him to find the cause of people's diseases and prophesize about society while in a hypnotic trance. There are now Edgar Cayce remedies, and his work inspired a whole new kind of alternative medicine. When Haley heard that Cayce suggested saffron as a treatment for psoriasis, she thought it may also be effective for atopic dermatitis and started drinking saffron tea. According to Cayce's explanation, psoriasis is not a problem of the skin, but a problem of the intestines. There are numerous tiny holes in the intestines that can allow proteins from food to enter the bloodstream, and this can be linked to inflammation of the skin. Saffron, Cayce claims, helps keep these tiny holes secure.

Haley did not see any sudden improvements, but after drinking the tea for six weeks, she noticed that when eating the foods she had been sensitive to, the reactions were much less pronounced.

> Now that is really unusual because once you have a food allergy, you have a food allergy... And you don't usually believe it... So I thought that's really good, it's amazing. That's amazing. So I carried on taking it, and yes, my food allergies got better. Not completely better. I'm still sensitive to milk and -- but, for example, this year, I've been very good at taking saffron regularly. I have no hay fever.

Haley then started taking fish oil and stopped eating meat completely. After two weeks, her atopic dermatitis disappeared completely.

> I stopped having meat, and I only had fruit and vegetables... For two weeks... I stopped itching, I could sleep at night, my skin felt more comfortable... It was amazing, and I thought, right, so I know it's not my skin. It must be what I'm eating.

At the time of the interview, Haley's skin was in such great condition that it was not apparent that she suffered from atopic dermatitis in any way. She says it was by changing her eating habits that she was able to cure it. Her understanding of atopic dermatitis differs drastically from that of modern medicine and is instead based on the holistic philosophy of alternative medicine. It is also backed by her interest in Edgar Cayce, naturopathy, yoga and meditation, healing crystals, and spirituality. Haley was still in school during the hippy movement of the 1960s, but she nonetheless describes herself as a 'later hippy.' From an early age, she has been exposed to the values shared by alternative medicine and hippyism. This philosophy is expressed in the way she seeks out treatment by herself, rather than relying on modern medicine.

Although she had used topical steroids for her entire life, she stopped when she was 35 and has maintained a symptomless state ever since. Even before she turned 35, she was unhappy about continually using steroids, but the relapse was so severe when she attempted to stop using them that she was forced to start using them again. However, when she turned 35, and the success of her dietary adjustments improved her symptoms, the need to continue using steroids gradually disappeared, and she was finally able to stop using them without relapsing.

As a result of using steroids for over 30 years, her skin had thinned significantly, and she said that this is not something that could ever be reversed, but it was not possible to tell simply by looking at her.

The interview lasted around an hour and a half, but there was additional time afterwards to continue chatting while I waited for my train home. Haley brewed some of the saffron tea she had discussed in the interview. She ground up a quarter of the saffron remaining in a small box with a pestle and mortar until it became a fine powder, and then she dissolved it in boiling water. She added the powder into a rainbow-coloured pot with plenty of hot water, which resulted in a pleasing yellow colour that almost seemed to shimmer. The tea was mostly odourless and tasteless, and very easy to drink.

After returning to the living room, Haley explained about chakras. The idea of a chakra is something that originated in India, and refers to energy nodes that can be found at several positions on the body, such as the head or abdomen, and are seen to glow blue or red. On that day, Haley was wearing a turquoise jumper and jeans, and a necklace decorated with turquoise, amethyst, and red stones. According to her explanation of chakras, the light blue or turquoise matches the chakra for the thyroid, and since she has a weak thyroid, she chooses to wear this colour. Judging from her belief in chakras, perhaps all of the objects and colours she had chosen to surround her also had some special significance. It could have been that the blue of her Nissan car, the turquoise of the jumper she was wearing, and the red of her sofa all had such significance.

As my train departure time drew near, Haley was in the middle of her explanation of chakras, and it was difficult for her to bring it to a conclusion. Her husband then approached suddenly and listened to the conversation beside her. When Haley came to a break in her story, her husband commented that I might miss my train. His perfect timing brought the conversation to a close just as I began to worry about leaving on time. When I asked Haley how he managed to come to the rescue with such perfect timing despite knowing nothing of the departure time, she replied with a smile, 'He has his own special sense, too.'

## Notes

1  The two Japanese interviewed in the UK (Michiaki and Michie) are also included in Table 4.1.
2  Osteopathy is a form of complementary medicine created by the American physician Andrew Taylor Still in 1874. It is based on the idea that the musculoskeletal system and visceral function are closely linked. Its aim is to heal a variety of ailments through manual adjustments to the musculoskeletal system.

## References

Arai, M. 1994, *Kōkoku no Shakaikeizaishi (The socio-economic history of advertisement)*, Tokyo: Tōyō Keizai Shinpōsha.

Cant, S. & Sharma, U. 1999, *A new medical pluralism?: alternative medicine, doctors, patients and the state*, London: UCL Press.

Charman, C. R., Morris, A. D. & Williams, H. C. 2000, "Topical corticosteroid phobia in patients with atopic eczema", *British Journal of Dermatology*, vol. 142, no. 5, pp. 931–936.

Fuller, R. C. 1989, *Alternative medicine and American religious life*, Oxford: Oxford University Press.

Gennep, A. V. 2004, *The rites of passage*, London: Routledge.

Ikeda, M. 1995, "Hi-seiyō iryō (Non-western medicine)," In Kuroda, K. (ed.) *Gendai Iryō no Shakaigaku (Sociology of modern medicine)*, Kyoto: Sekai Shisōsha, pp. 202–224.

Moynihan, R., Heath, I. & Henry, D. 2002 "Selling sickness: the pharmaceutical industry and disease mongering", *BMJ: British Medical Journal*, vol. 324, no. 7342, pp. 886–891.

Muraoka, K. 2000, "Minkan iryō no anatomy (Anatomy of folk medicine)", In Satō, J. (ed.) *Bunka Genshō toshite no Iyashi: Minkan Iryō no Genzai (Healing as a cultural phenomenon: the current status of folk medicine)*, Osaka: Medicus Shuppan, pp. 37–76.

Potter Drug and Chemistry Corporation. 1904, "Eczema: The world's greatest skin humour. Affects every age and condition. The only sure cure is Cuticura", *Essex Newsman*, 9 April, p. 3.

Takehara, K. 2000, *Atopī Business (The atopy business)*, Tokyo: Bungeishunjyū.

Thomas, K., Fall, M., Parry, G. & Nicholl, J. 1995, "National survey of access to complementary health care via general practice", viewed 7 March 2012, www.shef.ac.uk/content/1/c6/07/96/92/MCRU%20access1%201995.pdf.

Tsujiuchi, T. 2004, "Post-modern iryō ni okeru modern: hokan daitai iryō no jissen to senmonshokuka (Modern in post-modern medicine: practice and professionalization of complementary and alternative medicine)", In Kondo, H. & Ukigaya, S. (eds.) *Gendai Iryō no Minzokushi (An ethnography of contemporary medicine)*, Tokyo: Akashi Shoten, pp. 183–224.

Zollman, C. & Vickers, A. 1999, "ABC of complementary medicine: complementary medicine and the patient", *BMJ: British Medical Journal*, vol. 319, no. 7223, pp. 1486–1489.

Zwicky, J. F. & American, M. A. 1993, *Reader's guide to alternative health methods*, Chicago: American Medical Association.

# 5 The popular sector
## Self-help groups

### Atopy-free.com: a Japanese self-help group

*Background and policies*

Atopy-free.com is a self-help group run by staff who are themselves patients attempting steroid withdrawal. In 2015, there were about 20 staff members and 200 members paying an annual fee. The staff members run Atopy-free.com on a voluntary basis, as they also have other jobs. I first learnt of this group in 2006, after I learnt of and participated in Atopy Forum, an event held at Toyotomi Hot Spring in Hokkaido, Japan, where patients and doctors gave talks. The organizer of the event was Naoko Andō, who was acting as the main representative of Atopy-free.com. Naoko had received funding from the Takagi Fund for Citizen Science to conduct surveys on adult atopic dermatitis patients. The results were published in 2008 as a book titled *Atopīseihifuen Kanjya 1000 Nin no Shōgen* (*The Voices of 1000 Atopic Dermatitis Patients*). I was able to meet Naoko at the forum, and I learnt of Atopy-free.com through her.

Atopy-free.com was founded in 2005, and the driving force behind the organization's foundation was a petition started by patients who had begun steroid withdrawal in 2004. In order to have the side effects of topical steroids officially recognized, this group of patients acquired the domain Atopy-free. com to help them begin collecting signatures online. They presented their petition to the Ministry of Health, Labour and Welfare in 2005, and after this, Atopy-free.com was founded as a self-help group. Naoko co-founded this group with one of the people involved in collecting the signatures, Satoru, whose case study follows in this chapter. The group was thus named after the domain used for the petition.

Coming from this background, Atopy-free.com as a group maintains that steroids have side effects and thus promotes steroid withdrawal treatment. Since it is a group centred on the patients of steroid withdrawal doctors, these doctors are also heavily involved. A number of steroid withdrawal doctors attend almost every event, lecture, and forum that Atopy-free.com organizes. In recent years, patients have been very active in running and deciding the focus of events, but the influence of steroid withdrawal doctors is also recognized to an extent.

Atopy-free.com exists in a landscape of various types of patient self-help groups in Japan. These self-help groups can first be categorized according to level of professional involvement: groups with the significant involvement of professionals on one end of the spectrum and groups with significant non-professional member autonomy on the other. The former are primarily run, led, and funded by professionals, whereas the latter maintain some distance from professionals and are run mainly by patients themselves. I would put Atopy-free.com roughly midway between the above two ends of the spectrum. Although the group is run by patients, almost all of the staff are patients of steroid withdrawal doctors, and their way of thinking has been strongly influenced by these professionals. Furthermore, steroid withdrawal doctors participate in the planning of events or lectures, and they make appearances at events themselves. Such self-help groups run by doctors and patients together are quite rare, and perhaps one of the reasons it has been possible in the case of Atopy-free.com is the way that steroid withdrawal treatment brings doctors and patients closer together. In mainstream medicine, there is no need for a strong doctor–patient bond, but in steroid withdrawal treatment, doctors and patients are united in their collective fight against standard treatment. It could be said that this bond has led to the formation of a group run not by doctors or patients, but one that operates with their joint effort.

This cooperative relationship has also influenced the direction of the group. It has only been since the Second World War that self-help groups have formed as organizations in Japan. The earliest groups aimed to improve poor conditions faced by patients, overcome social stigmas and prejudices, or achieve other tangible goals. However, from the late 1960s to the 1970s, self-help groups began forming as organizations that offered psychological support to patients who suffered with similar problems by providing them with a way to share their experiences or by allowing them to exchange practical information that could directly solve their problems (Ukigaya, 2004). Atopy-free.com aims to bring about change by challenging the failure of the medical community to recognize the side effects of topical steroids, and, in this sense, it shares a lot in common with the older self-help groups. However, it also functions as a platform for patients with similar problems to share experiences and information, which means it has much in common with the more modern self-groups too. The influence of steroid withdrawal doctors is reflected, to some extent, in the Atopy-free.com's efforts to have the side effects of steroids recognized officially by society, whereas patients seem more interested in sharing their experiences and exchanging information. This is reflected clearly in the content of the lectures and forums organized or supported by Atopy-free.com. The group organizes both steroid withdrawal doctors' lectures and patient-centred forums. Whereas the lectures focus on the doctor and detail steroid withdrawal treatment, the forums centre on patients and facilitate information-sharing regarding lifestyle matters, such as how to maintain a job or how to relocate to Toyotomi Hot Spring in Hokkaido.

One event held in 2011, *Atopic Dermatitis Symposium: Rethinking Modern Atopic Dermatitis Treatment – Maximizing Your Natural Healing Potential without the Use of Steroids or Moisturizers,* exemplifies the doctor-centred aspect of the group. At this event, there were lectures from five steroid withdrawal doctors about their treatment, a lecture by Naoko Andō from the patient perspective, and a debate session. The aim of this event was to promote steroid withdrawal treatment, and it thus privileged the role of steroid withdrawal doctors.

In contrast, the group's forums centre on themes concerning day-to-day life rather than treatment. Another event, *The Atopy Forum in Tokyo 2011,* epitomizes this difference, in its theme of 'working life.' The first part consisted of three patients giving real examples of how they managed in their working life, the second was a panel discussion among patients, and the third part was a workshop for self-analysis. Three steroid withdrawal doctors attended this event, but the Atopy-free.com staff did not provide them with a chance to speak. Only patients were allowed to contribute, making it a forum for patients by patients. Such a patient-oriented forum demonstrates that the interests of patients often lie in exchanging information regarding everyday life rather than in treatment practices.

Atopy-free.com also publishes a newsletter three times a year. The newsletter is aimed at patients, and it is generally produced by staff members who are themselves patients. Much like the forums, it provides a way for patients to exchange information and offer support to each other.

By having steroid withdrawal doctors and patients work together in this way, Atopy-free.com allows both groups to promote their interests in tandem. Doctors are able to spread awareness about steroid withdrawal treatment, and patients are able to exchange information and share their experiences.

### Treatment goals

In Chapter 2, we saw how groups in each sector have different aims for treatment. The aims of the self-help group Atopy-free.com parallel those of steroid withdrawal doctors, namely, to stop the use of steroids and to cure atopic dermatitis. This comes through in the interviews I conducted with three staff members of the group: Wataru, Satoru, and Yukie. While they were unsure about whether they would ever actually cure their condition, their desire for a cure was evident in their answers.

> I may not be able to recover fully, but I feel like it's possible to recover maybe 80 or 90 percent. Like with my allergies, I've eliminated each factor that causes them one by one, so I'm decreasing my own negative factors one at a time. So, though it may take time, I definitely feel that I'm heading in a positive direction.
>
> (Wataru, 30, male)

> I think I might be able to recover. I have to believe that... I might not be able to, but there is just a chance that I will. So, it can trigger something.

The disease is the same. I think things get better when you have something to hold on to.

(Satoru, 38, male)

If I'm asked by a distressed patient if they'll recover, I tell them they will, and if researchers argue about whether or not it's possible, I ask them to work harder and investigate this.

(Yukio, 39, female)

I also felt the desire of the group for a complete cure when I attended the 2007 Atopy Forum in Tokyo. The forum hosted a patient-oriented workshop titled *Atopic Medical Care: What Are People Doing?* Part of the workshop involved participants forming groups to write down and present their thoughts on atopic dermatitis to each other. One of the most memorable things about this session was that one of the examples of things doctors said that hurt them was, 'Your atopic dermatitis can never be cured,' whereas one of the examples of things doctors said that made them happy was, 'Your atopic dermatitis can be cured.'

The steroid withdrawal doctors involved with Atopy-free.com generally see atopic dermatitis as a curable condition, and convincing patients they can recover provides peace of mind and emotional support that can aid in recovery. What was apparent at the workshop was that patients, too, want doctors to tell them they can be cured, and that this provides them with great encouragement. Steroid withdrawal treatment is a trying ordeal, and it is incredibly difficult to continue without the hope of a future recovery. In the midst of a severe relapse that can last months or even years, the promise of recovery from a doctor undoubtedly provides great reassurance.

There is, however, a downside of convincing patients that they can be cured. Zollman and Vickers (1999: 1487) point out that alternative medicine provides hope to patients, but they also emphasize that practitioners need to balance their claims carefully, considering the realistic chances of improvement and the dangers of creating false hope and further disappointment.

When confronting such a difficult disease, there is some possibility that the hope of a cure could improve a patient's ability to heal, but there is also the danger of the patient becoming depressed if a cure never comes.

[Case Study] Satoru (38, male): 'There are a lot of people in trouble, but they don't get the help they need.'

I met Satoru, an Atopy-free.com staff member, through Wataru, who was also involved with Atopy-free.com. When I asked Wataru if he knew any atopic dermatitis patients who would be willing to take part in an interview, Satoru was the first person he introduced. I interviewed Satoru once in 2006 and once in 2008. I also met Satoru occasionally through events and meet-ups hosted by Atopy-free.com. When we first met, Satoru was studying for a certificate related to law. By the time of his final interview, he had earned this certification and was looking for a job. He was constantly thinking ahead and trying to work out a way to maintain his job while managing his atopic dermatitis symptoms.

Satoru's first atopic dermatitis outbreak was in his third grade of elementary school. He was on the school baseball team, so it was especially noticeable when he gradually began developing symptoms on the hand he used to hold the ball, as well as on his arms and behind his knees. He had outbreaks around four times a year, and since his symptoms were especially bad when the seasons changed, he went to a hospital for a prescription of topical steroids during these times. His symptoms would disappear after around two weeks of applying the steroids, but they would flare up again after some time, and this cycle continued for several years.

Satoru first became completely reliant on steroids in his first year of high school, and his symptoms gradually declined with their use. Sometime after turning 20, however, his symptoms began responding less and less to topical steroids, no matter how often he used them. He started feeling uneasy about the quantity of steroids he was using and started to search for books on atopic dermatitis. In his search, he came across a book by the alternative medicine company Japan Ombas, which recommended hot spring therapy. Satoru grew worried and stopped using topical steroids based on the information in this book. A severe relapse followed, his symptoms peaking in severity a full month later. During that month, he was essentially bedridden, and he suffered symptoms across his entire body, even on the soles of his feet. Satoru was in his third year of university at this point, and he was absent from all classes except lab work.

By the time his symptoms next abated, Satoru was 23 and finally able to attend his classes. However, his condition gradually worsened over the next six months, and he was forced to suspend his studies altogether during his third year. He was able to return to university in his fourth year, when he immediately started looking for a job. He secured employment with a manufacturing company in a product management position. With his physical condition in mind, he chose a job that allowed him to finish at six o'clock and that involved only a 30-minute commute. Despite his best efforts, though, his body could not keep up with the demands of the job, and he was forced to resign after three months, when his symptoms flared up again. His condition steadily improved after leaving the company.

At 27, Satoru learnt of the steroid withdrawal doctor Dr. Yoshioka when he heard one of Yoshioka's lectures. When he was 28, he started playing table tennis again for the first time since high school. He practised hard enough to join a team and play in competitive matches. The sweating aggravated his symptoms for the first month, but after that, his symptoms recovered to the point that he felt 'amazing.' He then managed to find a new job within 40 minutes of his home and started to work again. He aspired for more from his career than the small company of only five employees could offer, so after a year and a half, he left this job for one at a medical centre.

After changing jobs, however, his symptoms again began to flare up. A doctor who both managed the centre and practised where Satoru worked provided him with a form of treatment that involved shoulder massages combined with laser diode treatment. He continued receiving this treatment while working there. However, he began feeling pressure from the doctor's efforts to cure him, and this, compounded with increased work stress, gradually worsened his symptoms.

Since his condition had declined to such an extent, Satoru arranged a consultation with Dr. Yoshioka. During the consultation, he decided to be hospitalized and asked Dr. Yoshioka to refer him to a hospital that would accept an atopic dermatitis patient. The idea of hospitalization was something he came up with to avoid having to quit his job when his symptoms became severe. Dr. Yoshioka introduced Dr. Akimoto (pseudonym), a doctor who carried out steroid withdrawal treatment in Osaka, and Satoru was admitted to his hospital at age 31.

After four weeks in Dr. Akimoto's hospital, Satoru's symptoms improved suddenly. Per standard treatment, the use of non-steroid creams or ointments is recommended in addition to steroids in order to moisturize the skin; however, Dr. Akimoto did not prescribe any of these. In fact, he guided his patients through ointment withdrawal, which actually dries out the skin. Whether due to ointment withdrawal or his release from the stress of working, Satoru's symptoms improved, and he was released from hospital after four weeks and soon returned to work. However, when he arrived at work, he realized he no longer had a job, and he was forced to quit after falling out with his manager.

For the next year and a half, Satoru recuperated at home while receiving accident and sickness benefits. During that time, he worked together with Dr. Yoshioka and others to collect signatures for an online petition to have the side effects of topical steroids officially recognized. This petition is what led to the foundation of Atopy-free.com as a self-help group. Satoru set up the website to collect signatures and worked for around two years as its representative.

During his recuperation period, Satoru also started studying for qualifications in the field of law. The reason he became interested in these qualifications was that he believed they would provide a means for him to work independently at his own pace. Since he had been using his disability benefit and unemployment insurance to survive without working, he also felt that knowledge of related laws would benefit him in the future.

Satoru continued studying for his exams while receiving unemployment insurance, and when that finally ran out, he worked part-time sorting belongings at a prison and supervising construction sites. He was finally able to pass his exams at age 35.

What stands out from Satoru's interviews is what a struggle it is for adult patients to maintain a job while trying to control their symptoms. For doctors, atopic dermatitis is only seen as a problem in terms of treatment, but for patients, it is a problem that affects every aspect of their lives. The fact that Atopy-free. com has hosted three forums on the theme of employment to date gives further indication of just how important this topic is to patients.

Satoru spoke of how difficult it was to find new jobs as he got older:

> I'm doing dispatch work right now. I feel like I'm falling further and further behind other people my age. I don't have many opportunities — both

in terms of pay and conditions. The more time that passes the worse off I become. It's hard. ... It gets harder and harder to find a job. The first job I found had the best benefits, and the second one I found at the job centre. Positions through the job centre don't have great benefits. ... With dispatch work, the pay itself isn't bad, but some amount of it is taken by the agency. Do you know how much they take? It's close to 40%. ... I'm not sure if dispatch work is even a good idea. ... It's not the kind of work you can just keep on doing.

Since Satoru has no option but to quit his job when his symptoms flare up, he cannot help feeling that he has entered a vicious cycle in which quitting one job makes finding the next one harder. He thus becomes increasingly disadvantaged compared to people his age who can work without problems. Satoru is all too aware of how suffering with atopic dermatitis drives so many patients to the bottom of the social ladder.

Atopic dermatitis isn't a disability, but recently I feel as though it creates problems that can be even worse than a disability. When I take a look at my CV, I really wonder if I'll be alright. I'm just not sure. It's really difficult when I have to explain it. I had an interview recently, and I was asked what kind of disease it is, and they rarely know it well. It's such a pain to explain it, since they just don't understand at all. It would help so much if people just understood it better. I wonder if anyone really cares about that. Since it's not a disability, there are a lot of people who can't get welfare benefits. There are a lot of people in trouble, but they don't get the help they need.

Satoru has had to quit his job multiple times when his symptoms flared up, and this is reflected in his CV. He speaks of how difficult it is to explain atopic dermatitis when looking for a job, since it is not a disease that people see as serious enough to necessitate quitting one's job. If it were classified as a disability, patients could receive easier access to welfare benefits and disability allowance, but since it is not, the number of options they have to fall back on is limited.

What stands out from Satoru's story is how difficult it is to live an independent life within society while dealing with atopic dermatitis. The aims of Atopy-free. com therefore include bringing together atopic dermatitis patients who endure these hardships and raising awareness in society of the side effects of topical steroids and the suffering of atopic dermatitis patients.

## The authorized NPO Atopicco Network for Children of the Earth: another Japanese self-help group

### Background and policies

I first came into contact with Atopicco Network for Children of the Earth in 2006. It was just after I had begun my investigation on atopic dermatitis, as

I was starting to attempt to contact self-help groups related to the disease. An Internet search revealed that Atopicco Network for Children of the Earth was an active group, and it was within a reasonable distance from my home in the Kanto region. I called their office and explained that I was researching atopic dermatitis and would like to attend one of the group's monthly patient meet-ups held in the evening. This was the beginning of my relationship with Atopicco Network for Children of the Earth.

When I visited the group's office in central Tokyo on the day of the meet-up, I was greeted by two of the directors, Tomomi Akagi and Jun Yoshizawa. They were responsible for actually running the group. Tomomi had shoulder length bobbed hair and wore loose-fitting clothes, and she explained things in a simple way with a smile. She is the mother of a child with atopic dermatitis. Since she is active in public-facing roles, such as lecturing and writing, she could be considered the face of the group. Jun has a gentle manner and had long, dyed-brown hair that was tied at the back. He does the accounting and other operations work, and generally anything he can to allow Tomomi to work effectively.

Tomomi and Jun agreed to allow me to observe events held by Atopicco Network for Children of the Earth over the long term, at least several years, and my relationship with the group has continued to this day. When I first started observing them, the group happened to be carrying out training for helpline counsellors, and my first involvement with the group was receiving this training and working as a volunteer helpline counsellor. After that, I had first-hand experience of seeing how the group operates in a variety of ways: members volunteered at summer camps for children, assisted in relocating the office, did one-off jobs, announced atopic dermatitis research, enjoyed end-of-year parties and evening dinners together, and travelled together.

The book *Atopī ni Katsu Network* (*Networks Overcoming Atopic Dermatitis*) by Hiromi Kanamaru details the history of Atopicco Network for Children of the Earth until 1995. According to the book, Tomomi's experience of raising her child in the 1980s led to the foundation of the group. Tomomi's child developed food allergies and atopic dermatitis at around the age of one, and eating eggs or dairy would lead to an outbreak of symptoms and cracked skin. As a result, Tomomi had trouble when her child began attending nursery school and was not able to eat the provided meals due to allergies. Tomomi suggested changes to the menu at the nursery, but it took a significant amount of effort to effect any changes. Nowadays, knowledge of children's food allergies has spread throughout society, and there is some level of general understanding. In the 1980s, however, there was little such understanding, and the nursery was not well equipped to deal with it. In the end, Tomomi had to go to the nursery kitchen before work and explain to the cook how to remove allergens such as eggs and soy. As a result, the nursery showed a willingness to improve their menus and followed Tomomi's suggestions.

As a result of her child's atopic dermatitis, Tomomi became interested in organizations such as the CO-OP and Seikatsu Club (Life Club), which could provide ingredients that she could use safely. From such groups, Tomomi came to know of Nihon Recycle Undō Shimin no Kai (the Japanese Recycling Movement Citizen's Council), a citizens' organization that aims to tackle environmental problems. It is also the parent organization of the organic vegetable delivery service Radish Bōya (Radish Boy). Tomomi called the Japanese Recycling Movement Citizen's Council and told them she would like to work for them. As part of the recruitment process, she was required to take an exam and write a report. She submitted a plan for a system to support mothers with children who suffer food allergies, a plan she had conceived based on her own struggles. It was enough to impress the recruiting manager, and Tomomi was hired.

Tomomi went on to become involved with many people through various research projects and screenings of films related to atopic dermatitis, which made her realize the importance of building a network. Kanamaru (1996: 110–111) quotes Tomomi on this:

> I struggled so much myself due to my child's allergies, but I didn't feel like joining parent or patient groups for children with allergies. I wanted something different. … I wanted to create a means of communication more than anything else. I wanted to help people build relationships more easily. I started off doing research and going to ecology school, and the idea of using the telephone came to me. I thought of starting off with simple phone calls.

From this, Tomomi went on to establish Atopicco Network for Children of the Earth within the Japanese Recycle Movement Citizen's Council, and this internal section focused on telephone consultations and the publication of a magazine. Tomomi explained that the group's name contains the following message:

> Children with atopy are sending a warning about the way people live. These children will carry the next generation to create a new way of living that is better in sync with the natural environment. These children themselves are the children of the earth.
>
> (Kanamaru, 1996: 112–113)

As can be inferred from this background, Atopicco Network for Children of the Earth could be seen as the product of the needs and doubts of one consumer, that is, one mother. It aims to provide society with an alternative that can gradually lead to change. This basic stance is very similar to the role played by the civilian sector, which is positioned as compensating for failures in the market or failures by the government (Ueno, 2011). Tomomi herself says of her motivation behind starting Atopicco Network for Children of the Earth: 'We need a fresh voice to talk to businesses and administrations' (Kanamaru, 1996: 110). In making suggestions from the citizen's perspective, which differ from both that of the government (administrations) and the market (businesses), the basic stance of Atopicco Network for Children of the Earth is clearly evident.

At the time of the Great Hanshin earthquake in 1995, the group helped to procure supplies for affected allergy patients and provide support at the disaster site. The extent of their efforts was summed up by Dr. Tomoyuki Chiba, who is closely involved with the group: 'What Tomomi and the others did went beyond volunteering. They showed selfless devotion. I was shocked by the extent of it' (Kanamaru, 1996: 189). Jun was also participating in the group's activities around this time.

In 1998, the parent organization of Atopicco Network for Children of the Earth, the Japanese Recycling Movement Citizen's Council, received approval from the Management and Coordination Agency to become an incorporated foundation, and subsequently became Nihon Kankyō Zaidan (the Japan Ecology Foundation). However, in 2002, the foundation announced an end to the operations of Atopicco Network for Children of the Earth, and all staff members were made redundant. In response, Atopicco Network for Children of the Earth became an independent organization and continued operating. It was recognized as a specified non-profit corporation (NPO) the following year and took on its current form.

Atopicco Network for Children of the Earth differs from various other self-help groups for atopic dermatitis in that Tomomi and Jun have made citizen activism their job, and they are able to make a living from it. In Japan, making citizen activism economically viable to this extent is fraught with challenges. Let us first look at the kind of activities Atopicco Network for Children of the Earth is involved in. According to its official website, it is involved in a wide range of activities, including a telephone helpline, environmental education camps, research, data releases, disaster site support, lecturer dispatching, and work with partners and subsidized projects. The telephone helpline has been active every Thursday and Friday since 1993. The camp is held every summer for people with allergies, and in recent years, the number of participants has grown to over 100, including volunteer staff. The research projects are designed, aggregated, and analysed in cooperation with researchers, health care workers, and experts before the data are finally released. In terms of supporting disaster sites, the group sent allergy supplies at the time of the Great Hanshin earthquake in 1995, the Great East Japan earthquake in 2011, and the Kumamoto earthquake in 2016. The lecturer dispatch involves Tomomi giving lectures on allergies and atopic dermatitis, and this happens around 20 times a year. The lecture topics include everyday life, signs of allergies, how allergies occur, everyday lifestyle considerations, the latest medical trends, the environment, chemicals, food, farming, raising children, breast milk, children, the body, the home, nature, society, education, gender, women, supporting disaster sites, developing new products, NPOs, and citizen activism. All of these activities are carried out by Tomomi, Jun, and a few other members, so they are constantly understaffed.

The cost of the group's activities was approximately ¥30,000,000 (£214,000 or $270,000) in 1995. However, since revenues covered only a third of that, the Japanese Recycling Movement Citizen's Council provided the remaining.

However, since the possibility of such subsidies disappeared when everybody was made redundant in 2002, they were then forced to raise funds themselves.

I attended a general meeting of Atopicco Network for Children of the Earth in 2008, and there I was able to get a sense of the group's management situation. In 2008, total revenues were at ¥12,000,000 (£85,000 or $109,000), and they were bearing a loss overall. Jun was not receiving any pay at all. At the meeting, they expressed the desire to avoid making Atopicco Network for Children of the Earth about money, and to do that, they would need to pursue a separate means of earning a living. However, it was pointed out that Tomomi and Jun already worked too hard and should respect the limits of their bodies. This shows that the more ambitious a citizens' association is in Japan, the harder it is for its members to continue making a living.

### Goals of the organization

Atopicco Network for Children of the Earth looks at atopic dermatitis from a very broad perspective that encompasses both environmental and societal issues, and their aim is not simply to find a cure for the disease. This excerpt from the official website, on a page titled *Towards Acceptance, Empathy and Tolerance*, illustrates their broader aims:

> It is our wish to provide atopy and allergy patients and their families with support and to create a society in which people and nature can coexist, diverse values are accepted, and everyone is able to live together in harmony.
>
> We hope for a balance between the body and mind, the environment and people existing together and prospering together, and freedom from itchiness, shortness of breath, and side effects of drugs and relapses. These are the things that everyone — people with allergic disorders, people with atopic dermatitis, people with asthma, people with food allergies, people with hay fever, healthy people, little children and big children, and adults — wishes for. How can we achieve this? What can the individual do to help? Atopicco Network for Children of the Earth wants to find answers and implement solutions.
>
> (Atopicco Network for Children of the Earth, 2012)

While it is difficult to understand the goals of the group clearly from the information on the website alone, I was able to learn much more through my interactions with Tomomi and Jun. According to Tomomi, her goal when she first founded Atopicco Network for Children of the Earth was to help provide the facilities necessary for people suffering with atopy, asthma, and so on to live as comfortably as normal people do. As already mentioned, unlike other children, Tomomi's child had food allergies, and so was not able to eat the same school meals as other children. Tomomi's goal was to develop a society that allows people who are not normal in this way to live the same way as others do. This goal overlaps with Tomomi's efforts to allow her child to experience school meals like any other child, rather than eating allergen-free meals from a special lunchbox. Tomomi spoke directly to the kitchen staff, as mentioned earlier, and would have them alter the meals in clever ways to avoid allergens and thereby enable her child to eat together with the other children. For example, they would make a vegetable omelette without eggs by frying the vegetables and sticking them together with potato starch, or they would boil curry ingredients and leave some aside for a soup before the curry powder was added (Kanamaru, 1996). The basic stance of Atopicco Network for Children of the Earth is evident in this desire to have something that is not typical recognized by society and to have a wider range of values accepted.

The group also wants atopic dermatitis to be seen as not just a problem of skin care, compliance, and topical steroids—as health care workers often believe—but as a result of wide-ranging factors that include the environment, the body, food, gender, and family. The following principles were outlined in a foreword to Tomomi's report for the Environment and Allergy Forum held in 1993:

1    It has been proposed that a true cure for allergies cannot be found until allergies are recognized as an environmental problem.
2    Allergies are caused by multiple factors. The causes include not only air pollution, but also food additives, pesticides, and high-protein and high-calorie diets, and these factors need to be considered along with their solutions.
3    Water pollution due to synthetic detergents and organic solvents does not just damage the environment, but also leads to residual chlorine, and can be a trigger for atopy symptoms (Kanamaru, 1996: 199–200).

As the aforementioned text plainly shows, at Atopicco Network for Children of the Earth, allergy disorders such as atopic dermatitis are seen as an environmental problem, not just diseases to be considered in a medical setting. This stance no doubt differs significantly from that of groups in other sectors, including standard treatment, alternative medicine, steroid withdrawal doctors, and the self-help group Atopy-free.com.

In addition, Atopicco Network for Children of the Earth sees atopic dermatitis holistically as a problem involving the entire body, rather than just symptoms on the skin. When I was speaking with Tomomi and Jun, we spoke of a past event held by the group about breast milk. This was about a breast massaging technique that can improve the production of breast milk. A woman acting as a model lay on a table to demonstrate the massage. As her body relaxed, a slight squeeze was enough for the milk to squirt out forcefully enough to almost reach the ceiling. It was an attempt to help people understand how wonderful the body can be. While discussing this topic, Tomomi noted that treating atopic dermatitis is undoubtedly important to the group, but she emphasized that she would also like people to understand that treatment is only one part of a larger whole. For Tomomi, the breast milk story was highly relevant to atopic dermatitis. She spoke of believing that everything, including the wonders of the body, could lead back to atopic dermatitis. From this it could be said that Atopicco Network for Children of the Earth is concerned not simply with whether or not topical steroids are used or even with curing atopic dermatitis, rather, its goal is for people to look at the disease in a much broader sense.

One also gets a sense that a further goal of Atopicco Network for Children of the Earth is to foster independence among both patients and consumers. Tomomi spoke as follows about her motivation for starting the group:

> As I became more active, I began to believe that I had to become independent as a consumer. If there are only good and bad things in the world, then you need to have the ability to choose the good things. As long as you have that ability, you'll never be indecisive.
>
> (Kanamaru, 1996: 108)

The idea of providing consumers with the knowledge they need to make the right choices without being led astray applies equally well to atopic dermatitis. During my conversations with Tomomi and Jun, we also touched upon the topic of Atopicco Network for Children of the Earth as a self-help group. One such way that it functions as a self-help group is with Tomomi as a central figure for patients. This way of thinking overlaps with the strategy of several steroid withdrawal doctors and self-help groups, of putting charismatic figures in a central role to appeal to patients. However, Tomomi and Jun said they did not wish for Atopicco Network for Children of the Earth to operate in this way. This is because they believe that there is essentially no difference between patients depending on topical steroids and patients depending on Tomomi or a doctor. It became clear that the goal of the group was not to encourage dependence, but rather to help patients develop a level of independence that allows them to make their own judgements.

As a result, Atopicco Network for Children of the Earth is resolute in the belief that the ultimate decision of whether or not to use topical steroids rests with the patient, and it is not the group's place to say whether either choice is good or bad. However, since the group acknowledges the risks of topical steroids and encourages a way of living that is kind to both the environment and the body, patients who do not use topical steroids tend to be especially drawn to the group. Doctors and alternative medicine practitioners who carry out steroid withdrawal treatment generally put forward discontinuing topical steroids and curing atopic dermatitis as treatment goals, but Atopicco Network for Children of the Earth does not take the approach of promising cures to encourage patients, even if they are going through steroid withdrawal. This may be the group's way of handling those patients who ultimately will not recover, no matter how much they may believe otherwise. The group's telephone helpline has received calls from patients who were not able to find a cure through standard treatment or steroid withdrawal. Jun spoke of the calls as follows:

> Atopicco Network for Children of the Earth hears from patients who are unhappy with standard treatment, patients who are unhappy with alternative

medicine, and patients who are unhappy with steroid withdrawal doctors. For example, some patients say their symptoms didn't improve even when they saw a steroid withdrawal doctor. This group is here to help those people who have nowhere left to go.

In this way, Atopicco Network for Children of the Earth is focused on finding a way to help the people who have tried everything and still have not recovered.

As noted in the previous chapter, making patients believe they can recover and having them work towards such a goal come with the risk of leaving them even more depressed in cases that do not work out as hoped. Medical anthropologist Azumi Tsuge (2004) points out the disconnect between patients' perceptions and a model of health care that only pursues treatment through research into cutting-edge medical technology.

> When fighting a disease, even committing a large amount of energy and money does not necessarily lead to a cure or any improvement. ... The idea that it is all about a cure leaves the lingering doubt that people with incurable diseases, people not seeking a cure, people who forgo treatment, and people choosing alternatives become increasingly isolated. ... It raises the concern that technological progress does not increase the options available to patients, but instead does nothing more than limit them to the choice of working towards a cure.
>
> (Tsuge, 2004: 161)

As Tsuge points out, the goal of health care is to cure the disease that patients suffer from, but for the patients themselves, treatment makes up just one part of their everyday life. There are even patients who try to prioritize other things ahead of their recovery. This is where the disconnect between patients and doctors occurs. This kind of disconnect is also evident in the case of atopic dermatitis. For some of these patients, there are more important things than curing their disease. Tomomi describes the viewpoint of patients who are not fixated on curing themselves:

> Should people suffering with a disease devote their entire life to it? Aren't there also cases where a cure is not necessary, where it's possible to live your life while receiving treatment, or where you continue living your life despite your disease?
>
> (Akagi, 2005: 108)

It could be argued that another of the aims of Atopicco Network for Children of the Earth is to open up the possibility of more diverse ways of living, rather than patients limiting themselves to the idea of a cure. This way of thinking also influences patients involved with the group. Kanae's case provides an example of this.

[Case Study] Kanae (32, female): 'Atopic dermatitis is just atopic dermatitis. It'd be nice to cure it, but that's about it.'

I first met Kanae through Atopicco Network for Children of the Earth, and we worked together as volunteers for the telephone helpline and the summer camp. Despite having a full-time office job, she has helped out significantly as a volunteer and developed a close relationship with the group. I interviewed Kanae twice, in 2007 and then in 2011.

Kanae was diagnosed with atopic dermatitis at around the age of two, and she has lived with the disease ever since. However, she gives no impression that it bothers her and seems to accept her condition for what it is.

For as long as she can remember, Kanae has applied the topical steroid Rinderon to the dry areas on her forehead. When she was seven, she went to the United States due to her father's work. She visited a Japanese doctor before leaving for the USA to get topical steroids. She remembers being surprised when he told her there was a high chance that her own children would also suffer with skin conditions, and that she shouldn't marry anyone with a skin condition. At that time, a yellowish liquid was oozing from the cuts on her scalp, so even though she was using topical steroids, she was still experiencing some level of symptoms.

When she returned to Japan from the USA as a junior high school student, she started going to a dermatology clinic by herself on the way home from school to get her topical steroids. Perhaps thanks to the fact that she was on the track and field team and exercised every day while leading a healthy lifestyle, her atopic dermatitis symptoms appeared only occasionally, and she was able to manage them by simply applying topical steroids to her forehead.

Soon after entering high school, Kanae enrolled in an exchange programme to study in the USA. When she went to the clinic before leaving the country, she was told that she could only be prescribed two weeks' worth of topical steroids, and this is what she took with her. Since she had to make two weeks' worth of medicine last a year, she used it only when absolutely necessary. In fact, her symptoms appeared only slightly in the first week and she recovered soon thereafter, allowing her to make it through the year with just two weeks' worth of medicine.

When Kanae returned to Japan, however, symptoms appeared on her face, on her forehead, and around her eyes and mouth, and she occasionally had to miss school. The reason for the flare-up was not clear, but she believes the reverse culture shock of returning to Japan, her relationships with friends and teachers, and studying for university entrance exams may have all had an impact.

When she entered university, she wore make-up only when absolutely necessary, since applying foundation usually aggravated her skin. In her third year of university, she decided to take a break to study abroad in China. As when she went to the USA, she took only two weeks' worth of medication with her to China, but when it ran out there, her face quickly became red. A friend introduced her to some cream containing Chinese herbal medicine, and she managed to get by using only this. She was also able to see a doctor who practised traditional Chinese medicine, and this made her doubt the symptomatic treatment of Western medicine. In turn, she started thinking that she may be better off trying to improve the overall health of her entire body, rather than continuing to rely on Western medicine.

> I'd always thought I could go to university, join a relatively well-established company, and lead a happy life. And get married and have kids and such. But following a set path isn't fun, and I felt like maybe I could pick my own path instead and start my life over. Even with food, I'd never actually looked at the ingredients before that. … But when I was in China, I began to prioritize my physical health.

Although she said she had never been particularly aware of what she was eating until she went to China, Kanae has been very conscious of her body and diet since then.

When returning to Japan, she told the doctor who had cared for her for ten years that she would like to try to improve her lifestyle rather than continuing to be dependent on drugs, and she had him introduce another doctor who would prescribe herbal medicine. She started living by herself around that time and tried to follow a lifestyle that put faith in the natural healing power of her body. She ate a diet of mostly vegetables without meat and snacks, used ginger and citrus rather than medicine when she caught a cold, and was careful to get enough sleep each night.

Kanae began looking for a job in her third year of university. Learning to wear a suit while fighting the urge to scratch when her make-up aggravated her skin, she managed to get through her interview and received an offer from the first company she visited.

When she joined her company, Kanae began steroid withdrawal. She had read a newsletter published by Atopicco Network for Children of the Earth that detailed the dangers of topical steroids, and this was what motivated her to try it. She experienced a severe relapse, which may have been worsened by a training exercise that involved handling chemical products, but she did not take leaves from work.

Kanae took a trip to Cambodia when she was 26. She had just changed departments at this point, and the increased workload impacted her health to the extent that dizziness and back pain required her to take time off work. However, going to Cambodia helped her change her mindset, and she was able to return to work soon after.

> I became able to let it go. I didn't think I was getting anything out of working so very hard. … I don't think you should live to work, I think you should work to live, and I think that enjoying life is more important. … I didn't need to put my job first, and I didn't need to work that hard. I started to get my priorities straight.

It appears that taking a step back from ideas of competitiveness and putting work first, along with focusing on things like her body and diet, laid the groundwork for her doubts about continued steroid use and pushing her body to its limits. She decided to make an effort to instead live naturally together with her symptoms. Although not using steroids means that her symptoms fluctuate, Kanae believes in accepting this and learning to live with it. In fact, for the past eight years, she has used steroids very little and has continued to take the good and bad times in stride.

Although there are people who believe they will find a cure through steroid withdrawal, and do their best to achieve this, Kanae does not give the impression of somebody who feels desperate to cure herself. When asked if she thought her atopic dermatitis would ever be cured, she answered,

> Atopic dermatitis is atopic dermatitis. It'd be nice to cure it, but that's about it.

Kanae thus was not attempting to cure her atopic dermatitis, but was trying to accept her disease for what it is. Kanae contributed to the Atopicco Network for Children of the Earth publication *Atopīseihifuen no Taiken wo Kataru: Otona ni Natta Kanjyatachi (Atopic Dermatitis Experiences: The Patients Who Grew Up)*, which recounted experiences of adult atopic dermatitis patients. She wrote the following in her contribution:

> I don't really know if atopic dermatitis can be cured or not. I'd be happy if it could be, but I wouldn't go to any lengths to make it happen, because atopic dermatitis is a part of me too. Instead of sacrificing everything and tying myself down for the sake of a cure, I think I would rather live an easier, more relaxed life, even just a little.

> (Akagi, 2006)

This kind of outlook overlaps somewhat with the goals of Atopicco Network for Children of the Earth.

## The National Eczema Society: a British self-help group

### Background and policies

In the previous section, the self-help group Atopy-free.com and Atopicco Network for Children of the Earth were presented as examples of what can be found in the popular sector in Japan. These two groups either stand opposed to standard treatment or attempt to distance themselves from it. Although they were not covered as part of the research for this book, other groups that are supported by doctors practising standard treatment, such as the authorized NPO Japan Allergy Tomono Kai (Japan Allergy Friends Group), also exist.

Conversely, when I searched for self-help groups in the United Kingdom, I could only find one: the NES. The NES, like Japan Allergy Tomono Kai, is a self-help group that promotes standard treatment. The NES is presented in leaflets produced by the BAD and promoted as a source of information through the likes of the NHS. What is clear from this is that the NES represents modern medicine, and it is recognized by society as a legitimate self-help group. The group had 4,500 members as of 2010, and the yearly membership fee was £20 for British residents and £40 for those living overseas.

The NES engages in a range of activities, such as running a telephone and e-mail helpline, publishing their quarterly magazine, *Exchange*, as well as various leaflets and booklets, contributing to research into eczema treatment, providing education and training to health care professionals, and providing access to a network of local support groups.

I joined the NES in 2009, and I was able to see how the group operates by receiving copies of the quarterly magazine *Exchange* along with leaflets and booklets, attending the general meeting in 2010, and attending monthly regional support groups where patients share their experiences. In addition, though I was not a member at the time, I was able to attend a training session titled Study Days for Healthcare Professionals in 2008.

Based on the aforementioned experiences, one of the most noticeable differences between the NES and self-help groups in Japan is that the NES is in a position to provide education not only to patients, but also to professionals. This applies to the Study Days for Healthcare Professionals training sessions mentioned earlier and to various other Study Days training sessions held across the UK. In 2012, six Study Days sessions were held across the UK in six locations, including Manchester, Birmingham, and London. The Study Days session I attended in 2008 was held in Manchester, and it went from morning until afternoon, with lunch and tea breaks in between. The session consisted of presentations by both health care professionals and patients on the topic of caring for patients with eczema. The guidelines distributed there were produced in cooperation with the BAD and the Primary Care Dermatology Society (PCDS) and ultimately followed the guidelines of mainstream medicine.

One of the more memorable points of the session was a presentation clearly emphasizing that eczema could not be cured. Since stressing the lack of a cure directly to patients can leave them feeling dejected, it is common to focus on how the disease can be effectively controlled, but these considerations were perhaps unnecessary there, since the session was aimed at health care professionals. There was also a scene that the organizers could not have foreseen. While discussing the side effects of topical steroids, one of the speakers showed a picture of a patient with severe thinning of the skin, to the point that it had split open at several points on the body. Since the picture was graphic and hard-hitting, one of the organizers hurriedly tried to dismiss it as a rare occurrence. The position of the organizer hinted at the way the NES attempts to educate health care professionals to allay concerns surrounding topical steroids and ensure that the medication is used properly. When the presentations were over, each participant was given a certificate to show that they had participated in Study Days.

The self-help groups that I investigated in Japan were all focused on patients, and there were no examples of providing education to health care professionals. In contrast, rather than being run in the shadow of health care professionals, the

NES is in a strong position to provide mainstream treatment education to both patients and health care workers.

### Treatment/activity goals

A look at their quarterly magazine, *Exchange*, makes it clear that the NES promotes mainstream modern medicine. The types of treatment covered are exactly the same as those introduced in the professional sector. What makes *Exchange* interesting is that each edition contains patient stories, and through these stories, it is possible to get a sense of what type of patient is seen as ideal and to contrast this with the ideal in Japan.

In Japan, whether the stories are of patients receiving standard treatment or those receiving alternative medicine treatments, the majority ultimately show the patient regaining beautiful skin and being able to lead a happy lifestyle. For example, there was a series of features published in the *Asahi Shimbunr* 9–14 November 2010 titled *Kanjya wo Ikiru: Otona no Atopy* (The *Lives of Patients: Adult Atopy*). The story of Miwako Ogino, 31, was introduced as an example of a patient who saw improvement in her symptoms through standard treatment. She had suffered from atopic dermatitis from an early age and had begun steroid withdrawal treatment in her fourth year of university. For the following five and a half years, while seeing no improvement in her condition and enduring terrible symptoms, she stopped using topical steroids and continued to believe her atopic dermatitis would be cured. However, on her family's advice, she went for a consultation at Tokyo Teishin Hospital, and reluctantly began treatment involving topical steroids. Her symptoms were under control within a few days, and she was able to maintain a stable condition thereafter (Suzuki, 2010).

Similarly, examples involving alternative medicine can be seen in the free magazine *Atopy Navi* published by Japan Ombas, which includes patient stories in each edition. Each of these stories follows a similar pattern in which the patient stops using topical steroids and goes on to recover from their atopic dermatitis through the hot spring therapy provided by Japan Ombas.

Unlike the Japanese stories of patients overcoming atopic dermatitis, the stories included in *Exchange* do not necessarily always have a happy ending in which the patient recovers. They instead tend to have a common theme of patients having to live with their symptoms, but nevertheless trying hard and managing everyday life. As an example, the story of Angeline Fowler, which was published in the September 2010 edition of *Exchange*, will be introduced. The article starts as follows:

> Today I'm a respected professional with an advanced degree, a happy marriage, and a young daughter. But as I write this during my lunch hour at work, I desperately want to rip off my jeans and scratch the backs of my knees, my scalp is flaking and today it hurts to smile because the cracks at the side of my mouth are healing shut.
>
> (Fowler, 2010: 12)

As one can tell from the introduction, Angeline's story is not the type that shows improving symptoms leading to a happy ending. Angeline was born in 1970, and since doctors in the UK had no knowledge of eczema at the time, she was diagnosed with hives and did not receive appropriate treatment. Her symptoms were severe when she was very young, and she was given the nickname Spot; she found it hard to fit in. When she was eight, her father found an expert who was carrying out research on eczema, and had Angeline try dietary therapy at his clinic. At first, she was only allowed to eat turkey, rice, and pineapple, and she continued adding one new food to her diet per month for the next five years. Elementary school and secondary school were difficult times for Angeline. In particular, during secondary school, she wanted to stop using her coal tar shampoo, dye her hair, and be fashionable like everybody else. However, wearing eyeliner or having piercings only risked aggravating her symptoms, so her parents were very strict about such things. Angeline had little confidence due to her eczema, and she was not an outgoing person. When she turned 16, the eczema on her face cleared up, and symptoms remained only on her body. She managed to find a boyfriend but always questioned why he was interested in dating her; the relationship ended after two years.

Angeline's life changed after she graduated from sixth form college and went to study abroad in Alaska. Her eczema was visible only around her joints and on her back at the time, and it wasn't obvious looking at her that she suffered from the disease. She made friends there and met the man who would become her husband. Gaining his acceptance helped her to accept herself.

When Angeline became pregnant, her life changed once again. Her eczema returned, and symptoms reappeared on her face. After becoming pregnant, she stopped wearing make-up, using products for her hair, and wearing nylon or dry-cleaned shirts, since these were all triggers for her symptoms. Of course, the apparent decline in her appearance drew stares and comments from those around her, but she says that growing older and becoming a mother helped her to deal with these problems more effectively.

As she said at the start of the article, her symptoms certainly did not disappear, and she spoke of having good days and bad days, and even days when she did not want to get out of bed. Nevertheless, she had to fight the pain, get up, and make her way through another day. Her story presents a clear contrast to the happy endings featured in the Japanese stories; instead, it paints a picture of a woman living day-to-day with her eczema.

There are many potential explanations for the difference in the nature of patient stories seen in the UK and Japan. First, there are different motivations for telling these stories. Many of the stories in Japan act as propaganda for standard treatment, alternative medicine, or some other group. In particular, the hostility between the advocates of standard treatment and steroid withdrawal treatment in Japan leads to the two presenting success stories in order to promote the benefits of one over the other. Meanwhile, in the UK, there is no steroid withdrawal or other particular form of treatment that poses a threat to modern medicine.

As a result, there is little need for propaganda promoting modern medicine success stories over other forms of treatment.

Differences may also arise because the patient stories in *Exchange* are not third-person reportage, but first-person accounts by the patients themselves. Even given some level of editing, patients have a certain degree of freedom when writing about themselves.

From the way the patient stories are written, it is clear that what the NES is aiming to do is not to cure eczema, but instead to provide a platform for patients to come together and consider how they can better live with their disease. In the case of standard treatment in Japan, the impression given is that using topical steroids to control symptoms will prevent any chance of a serious flare-up. The NES, on the other hand, acknowledges the fact that patients will have to deal with some difficult days, which is more in line with what patients actually experience.

An NES booklet aimed at adult patients titled *A Members' Guide to the Management of Atopic Eczema in Adults* also has a different tone from that of standard treatment advocates and the popular sector in Japan. While the Japanese self-help group Atopy-free.com regularly raises the topic of how patients can manage their disease with their working life, the NES extends this advice on treatment and everyday life even further. In the booklets aimed at adult patients, there is not only advice on work-related topics, but also on physical intimacy, pregnancy, and old age, which are interesting additions not taken up to such an extent by Japanese self-help groups.

In terms of physical intimacy with a partner, the following are a few examples of the practical advice given by the NES:

- If you try to avoid physical or sexual contact with your partner because of how your skin feels, your partner may feel rejected. Explain how it makes you feel physically, what you like, and what gives you pain or causes itching, and try to reach some compromise.
- Share your skin care regimen with your partner and make it enjoyable.
- Some positions might be more comfortable than others if certain parts of your body are sore. Experiment together and discuss which positions you both prefer.
- Having a bath or shower immediately after intercourse can stop your skin becoming irritated. Explain this to your partner—don't just leap into the shower straight after sex without explanation (Jordan, 2003: 4–6).

The NES booklet mentions that during pregnancy, changes in hormones may have positive or negative effects on symptoms; low-potency topical steroids should be used during pregnancy, and use of higher potencies requires consultation with a physician; also, higher-potency topical steroids may be used within the first three months of pregnancy (Jordan, 2003).

Regarding eczema in old age, the booklet provides some advice for reducing varicose eczema: it is important to control your weight to avoid aggravating symptoms; you should periodically lie on a bed or sofa and elevate your legs; and if eczema should break out around the ankles, then you should wear support socks (Jordan, 2003).

Since the NES provides information and advice regarding not only treatment, but also the wide variety of problems patients may face in their everyday lives, it could be argued that the group views the disease in a much broader way than as something to be treated in a hospital. This is perhaps one of the benefits of operating as a self-help group. Although many aspects of the NES overlap with self-help groups in Japan, sexual problems are treated as taboo in Japan, and issues of old age have not yet been taken up. It therefore seems that the NES is prepared to be much more open with the information it provides.

NES support groups openly sharing such information can be found in regions across the UK, and I will next introduce some of these as cases. From 2010 to 2011, I participated in the Kingston and Richmond Eczema Support Group, which provides a place for patients to share experiences once a month. On days with low attendance, I was one of only four people present, while on other occasions there were 14 attendees. Participants discussed a wide range of topics, in addition to treatment, in the lobby of Kingston Hospital, from 8 to 10 PM. The organizer, Lulu O'Hagan,[1] was both an atopic dermatitis patient herself and the mother of a child with atopic dermatitis, and the two other regular attendees, Sue and Nicky, were also mothers of children with the disease. I took the following field notes during the June 2010 meeting:

> I arrived late this evening, after 9 PM. When I got to Kingston Hospital, as always, everyone was around the table, but the discussion was more heated than usual. The members in attendance were the regulars, Lulu, Sue, and Nicky, as well as a British man with his Korean wife and baby, and two British women in their 30s. Including me, there were eight adults. After around 30 minutes, one of the British women left for home, and the rest of us spoke until 10 PM. The other British woman appeared worried about her four-and-a-half-year-old child, who was suffering with eczema. She spoke of being against rubbing topical steroids into her baby's skin, and was only doing so where symptoms were visible, while the doctor was telling her to do it across the baby's whole body.
>
> The Korean woman was also uncomfortable about rubbing topical steroids into her eight-month-old baby's skin, and it seemed that the reason she had come was to ask for opinions. Just as I walked in she was claiming that using topical steroids was pointless, since the symptoms kept returning regardless. She became a little emotional and was tearing up as she finished speaking. According to Sue, when the woman's husband said the baby's symptoms were severe, the woman disagreed and started crying. Sue's view was that the woman, as the baby's mother, was desensitized to the symptoms, and it came as a shock to her that other people saw them as severe.
>
> The British woman speaking before also spoke of her shock when her baby was diagnosed with eczema. Sue's take on this was that given the idea

of babies having beautiful skin, when your own child develops the damaged skin of an atopic dermatitis patient, it can come as a shock and leave you with a feeling of having failed your child.

As the central members of the group, Lulu, Sue and Nicky were of the opinion that, despite their misgivings about doing so, it was necessary to properly rub topical steroids into their baby's skin. Lulu had argued to the British woman that she herself was an example of topical steroids being safe, since she had used them for years, and yet the skin on her fingers was fine. The British woman admitted to being concerned about topical steroids but felt reassured by meeting Lulu.

Sue told the Korean woman that she appreciated that she may be scared of using topical steroids, but that it was necessary to rub them in three times a day until the itchiness disappeared completely, and then stop using them for a while. Both the Korean woman and British woman seemed to come in the hope of having their fear of topical steroids allayed, and since the three regular women were in favour of steroids, I think they may have left feeling some discontent.

When the new members left at 10 PM, the four of us remained and continued talking. Everyone had got a little worked up and wanted to talk a little about the people who had come that day. Sue and Lulu felt that the Korean woman may not return. They felt it was hard to connect with her. Sue, on the other hand, said that such things were necessary for the group to function as a place for people to vent their pent-up stress. In that sense, she felt glad that the woman had come.

This excerpt from my field notes provides some sense of how many patients in the UK also feel uneasy about topical steroids, and it suggests that one role of the NES is to reassure patients that they can use topical steroids without fear. As we will continue to see, the position of the NES is ultimately to educate patients to adhere to the mainstream treatments of modern medicine.

Next, we turn to the story of the support group's organizer, Lulu.

[Case Study] Lulu (46, female): 'It made you feel that you want to be at the center of attention so that you can feel that you are liked.'

I first met Lulu at the NES support group described previously. She is a Caucasian woman in her mid-40s, with hair as short as an average man's and a slim build. Her eyes give the impression of a sharp astuteness, and she comes across as very intelligent. She is the mother of two children. It was hard to tell that she suffered from eczema just by glancing at her fair skin, but the scabs on her hands became apparent in our introductory handshake. What also became clear after speaking to her was that she had lost a lot of hair due to an onset of alopecia several months before and that it had finally just started growing back.

The meetings were always held in the lobby of Kingston Hospital, but on one occasion when Lulu could not find a babysitter and was therefore not able to leave her house, she hosted the meeting at her home. The members in attendance that day were only the two regulars, Sue and Nicky, and me. Lulu's house was large and comfortable, and it appeared she had an eye for design. The small, white flowers in bloom in the front garden made it feel like spring, and there were pink clematis growing next to the front door.

Lulu's hair had grown since our first meeting, and she was looking well. Her hair must have reached 5 cm, and it was curled as if she had had it permed. She wore black-framed glasses, a striped shirt with a black skirt, stockings, and a necklace that looked like numerous silver rings linked together. It was a lovely outfit that almost made her look ready to go out for the evening. She hugged Sue as she entered the front door, and then she shook my hand and welcomed me inside.

As we walked straight in, there was a large kitchen with a dining table on the left, and the living room was further in. Inside were two large sofas, a table, and a large flat screen TV, while the wall was covered with family pictures and paintings. Most of the pictures were of her two daughters, but there were also some of her and her husband. One of the pictures of Lulu in her younger years showed her looking beautiful with blonde hair. She told me that she did not experience symptoms on her face, and her beautiful pictures showed absolutely no signs of eczema.

Nicky soon came in with some tea, and when Lulu asked what the agenda was for the evening, I took the opportunity to ask to interview her, and she accepted. Sue and Nicky sat on the other sofa listening to Lulu's interview.

Lulu first developed eczema about three weeks after her birth and continued to suffer severe symptoms for some time. The disease led to her having a difficult childhood.

> Primary school was horrible. Only I and one other boy had eczema. I had only one main friend. I thought that senior school would be better because children are older, but there were still comments on it. I didn't have one main friend. Everyone was in twos, but I wasn't. I was always number three. I would sit on my own or with someone only if their friend was off ill. It took two to three years to find one person I could sit with.

She was not able to enjoy her school days, and she also suffered significant physical pain due to her eczema.

> So, it was very painful to work and I had a lot of homework because I was in the top sets. I often spent three hours doing my homework, and probably half of that time I was scratching. So, it would take me longer to do my work than a 'normal' child.

In addition to the pain eczema caused her body, she also suffered from the fact that her parents did not acknowledge it.

Because my mum and dad treated me like I was normal, I never realized, and therefore allowed for, how ill I really was. I have a lot of criticism of their parenting, even sending me 10 miles away to school was too much. There should have been allowances made for me. Then you don't realize to make allowances for yourself. Most days just to get out bed would be so painful, and then my mum would make me walk to primary school, which was a mile away. My legs were sore and stiff. She should have driven me but just hadn't thought through my actual pain. As mentioned, secondary school was 10 miles away and that involved a bus, a train, and then 20-minute walk. I remember the drought of 1976 when I was 13 – it was so hot. It was like torture getting there and back, and just generally every day with the heat.

Despite the unforgiving circumstances, Lulu continued going to school without being absent. When she was 14, she finally reached her limit. She was no longer able to attend school and went to stay with her grandmother in Durham for a month.

My mum said I had had a nervous breakdown, but I don't know if that is exactly what it was. I just couldn't cope any more with the daily grind of no sleep, bleeding on sheets, dealing with everyone else at school being 'normal' and trying to be liked and to be like them. Plus, I wanted to be away from my mother and father, who were really irritating. My mother was very, very strict, and I wanted to escape and rest with my lovely, kind grandma. She was great. She changed my sheets every day because every day they were covered in blood. It was cooler in Durham anyway. So it was probably better.

While she was in Durham, Lulu tried herbal therapy on her mother's recommendation. It was 1978, an era when nobody knew about alternative medicine. Lulu's grandmother took her to a herbalist, and she was given some floral remedies. When she tried taking it, the joints in her hands started to lock up, and she became unable to pick anything up. She thought it was a sign that she may be recovering, but her mother told her to stop the treatment at once after hearing her situation on the phone, and that is ultimately where it ended.

After graduating from secondary school, Lulu wasn't well enough to enter the sixth form college,[2] so her mother told her to go to a college for secretaries. She studied there for a year and went on to work as a secretary for two years. Working in an environment surrounded by adults was comfortable for her. She also tried homoeopathy around this time but failed to see any results.

After her job as a secretary, Lulu started work at the stock exchange, where there were only ten women but around 1,500 men. She laughed when recalling how kind the men were to the women. She worked there for six years, from age 19 to 25. Since she had symptoms on only her hands and not her face, she managed fairly well during that period.

In 1986, when Lulu was 23, there was a sudden deregulation of financial markets in the UK (the Big Bang). A news reporter from a television network came to her office to interview an employee at the stock exchange. Lulu's company saw her as a good candidate, and chose her to interview. The reporter told her that she was a good fit for TV and asked her if she had ever considered working in the industry. She had never thought about doing such a job, but the conversation sparked her interest. Since she was about to be made redundant by her company at the time, she decided to look for her next job in the TV industry.

Among the people interviewed for this book, there were some who said they felt confident in front of others, but many of them said it made them feel uncomfortable. When I asked Lulu if appearing on TV made her feel uncomfortable, she replied this way:

> I remember hearing a radio DJ, called Simon Bates, who was on Radio 1, and he said he was bullied at school for different reasons. It made you feel that you want to be at the centre of attention so that you can feel that you are liked. And I could understand that. But I wasn't conscious about that – I just knew that I wanted to do it. I have done some now, that was on cable channels, reviewing movies and things, and I was good at it. Because I know how to talk to the camera and look down the lens and because I've done floor managing and worked with presenters. But I don't do it now. I didn't succeed in that direction.

Lulu wanted to do a job that would involve being in front of a lot of people, such as a television presenter, but she said finding such a job was difficult. Six months after leaving the stock exchange, she found a job as an assistant floor manager at a TV company. This involved giving cues to presenters and camerapersons as part of floor management. From there she became a third assistant director, and then a second assistant director for films.

Lulu worked as a freelancer between the ages of 25 and 34. At 34, she became pregnant with her first daughter and focused mainly on being a stay-at-home mum, after marrying her husband, whom she met at work on a film. When asked about her husband's feelings towards her eczema, she answered as follows:

> He didn't mind. When you have eczema, you get the best boyfriends. Because they have to see through the horrible skin to see you and to be with you. They would see you naked and scratching sometimes, and would soothe you by tickling or stroking the skin to help you. I got the decent men. I had a very beautiful best friend for a long time who always got the lovely looking boyfriends. But I always felt that her boyfriends were more shallow.

Lulu gave birth to her second child two years and eight months after her first. Her second daughter had terrible eczema, and the itchiness stopped her from sleeping at night. Lulu herself was not able to sleep as a result, and this led to a flare-up of her own symptoms. At age 42, after going to Great Ormond Street Hospital, she agreed for her daughter to go on the immunosuppressant azathioprine and for herself to use ciclosporin under a consultant's advice. She said this relieved her asthma symptoms, and her itchiness resolved completely. However, ciclosporin has to be monitored with monthly blood tests. She stayed on them for five years. When she was not using ciclosporin, she controlled her symptoms with topical and internal steroid medications. When I asked if she was afraid of using topical steroids, she replied,

> Yeah, but if you ask which one do I prefer, I like taking in the results, and I prefer the steroids because even with steroids I don't get these crack things. Yeah, I do have fear ... osteoporosis.

And when I asked if she was afraid of using ciclosporin, she said,

> Not really. Because they monitor you, you have to have a blood test every four to six weeks to check your liver function and your blood, so I would fear it if it stopped working.

At the end of her interview, Lulu was asked if she had learnt anything from suffering with eczema, or if it was nothing but a difficult experience for her. Her answer was, 'If you asked if I would live this life again with eczema, I would say no.' With that, the interview was over.

Lulu's interview lasted around 50 minutes. It took a lot of energy for both Lulu and me to cover her life story, but Lulu was kind enough to answer the questions frankly. She was sharp-witted and eloquent and had clearly thought about eczema in depth. I had also dared to ask some relatively intrusive questions, but Lulu did not become offended or refuse to answer. She was nothing but cooperative. Perhaps her struggling with her disease and experiencing a life different from the average person had helped make her more accustomed to looking at her own life objectively.

## Notes

1 Information about eczema and the monthly support group organized by Lulu can be accessed at www.facebook.com/eczemasupport.
2 Sixth form college is for students aged from around 16–19 to learn advanced school-level subjects for two years in order to apply for university education.

## References

Akagi, T. 2005, *Allergy to Tanoshiku Ikiru* (*Living in harmony with allergy*), Tokyo: Gendai Shokan.

Akagi, T. 2006, *Atopīseihifuen no Taiken wo Kataru: Otona ni natta Kanjya tachi* (*Reliving atopic dermatitis: from patients who are now adults*), Tokyo: NPO Atopicco Network for Children of the Earth.

Andō, N. 2008, *Atopīseihifuen Kanjya 1000 nin no Shōgen* (*Testimony from 1000 atopic dermatitis patients*), Tokyo: Kodomo no Miraisha.

Atopicco Network for Children of the Earth. 2012, *Atopicco Chikyū no Ko Network ga Mezasu Mono (The goal of atopicco network for children of the earth)*, viewed 21 March 2019, www.atopicco.org/philosophy.html.

Atopicco Network for Children of the Earth. 2013, *Natsuyasumi Kankyō Kyōiku Camp (Environment education camp in summer vacation)*, viewed 21 March 2019, www.atopicco.org/activity/education/.

Fowler, A. 2010, "A life less ordinary: Angeline Fowler describes how lifelong eczema has shaped her life", *Exchange*, no. 137, pp. 12–14.

Jordan, S. 2003, *A members' guide to the management of atopic eczema*, London: National Eczema Society.

Kanamaru, H. 1996, *Atopī ni Katsu Network (Network for overcoming atopy)*, Tokyo: Kōsaidō Shuppan.

Suzuki, A. 2010, "Kanjya wo Ikiru: Otona no Atopy" (The lives of patients: adult atopy), *Asahi Shimbun*, 9 November, p. 35, 10 November, p. 33, 11 November, p. 29, 12 November, p. 34, 13 November, p. 33, 14 November, p. 33.

Tsuge, A. 2004, "'Naosu koto' wo meguru kattō: Sentan iryō no alternative nitsuite kangaeru (The dispute on 'cure': searching for an alternative for advanced medicine)", In Kondo, H. & Ukigaya, S. (eds.) *Gendai Iryō no Minzokushi (An ethnography of contemporary medicine)*, Tokyo: Akashi Shoten, pp. 123–163.

Ueno, C. 2011, *Kea no Shakaigaku: Tōjisha-syuken no Hukushi Shakai he (Sociology of care: toward a patient-centred welfare society)*, Tokyo: Ōta Shuppan.

Ukigaya, S. 2004, *Byōki dakedo Byōki deha nai: Tōnyōbyō to Tomoni Ikiru Seikatu Sekai (Sick but not sick: a life with diabetes)*, Tokyo: Seishin Shobō.

Zollman, C. & Vickers, A. 1999, "ABC of complementary medicine: complementary medicine and the patient", *BMJ: British Medical Journal*, vol. 319, no. 7223, pp. 1486–1489.

# 6 The controversy over patient knowledge

## Insights from a comparison between Japan and the UK

According to Arthur Kleinman (1988), illness narratives can be explained in terms of a triangular framework of cultural representations, collective experiences, and individual experiences. Cultural representations include issues such as what image people have of an illness in a particular place and era, the meaning the illness is given, and in what way the body is symbolized. Collective experiences refer to things such as the posture and gestures of the body that are shared within a given society and an understanding of what is valued within a given society. Individual experiences, as the term suggests, denote the experiences of the individual suffering with a disease (Kleinman, 1988).

When comparing the UK to Japan through this framework, the stories patients tell are surprisingly similar at the level of individual experiences. During the interviews, for example, patients in both the UK and Japan told stories with many overlapping themes, including bullying, conflicts with parents, a desire to be accepted by others, and problems communicating with others. From these individual experiences, one can see that atopic dermatitis patients from Japan and the UK share problems that go beyond the cultural issue. Moreover, contrary to my expectations, the way people perceive topical steroids is also very similar in the UK and Japan. Since the problems associated with topical steroids have been covered much more extensively in the Japanese media, it seemed natural to assume that the perception of topical steroids would be much more negative in Japan than in the UK. However, around half of the people in Japan had a negative view of topical steroids, and a similar trend emerged from my interviews in the UK. Looking at the data, it is difficult to believe that the negative perception held by individual patients is fuelled by the media, as is often said in Japan; instead, this perception seems to be a collective opinion that patients have formed through actually using the medication.

Despite these commonalities at the individual level, important differences become evident at the levels of cultural representation and collective experience. As mentioned in the first chapter, the level of attention given to atopic dermatitis and topical steroids in Japan is considerably higher than in other countries. This is similar to the way the MMR vaccine debate and RSI receive attention in the

UK but not in Japan, and this could be seen as an issue of cultural relevance. In the case of Japan, the consideration given to the side effects of topical steroids by the mass media and the alternative medicine industry was likely the direct cause of this difference. The idea of steroid withdrawal then gained popularity in Japan, and patient knowledge supporting it was able to develop. In the UK, on the other hand, the idea of steroid withdrawal does not even exist, despite the large number of patients with misgivings about topical steroids. This is further evidence that there is not necessarily a direct relationship between patients disliking topical steroids and steroid withdrawal emerging as a treatment. Why is it that a trend towards steroid withdrawal could be seen in Japan but not at all in the UK?

Firstly, as mentioned in Chapter 4, the way that alternative medicine is regulated could be a factor. Alternative medicine in Japan is, as Takuya Tsujiuchi (2004: 212) expressed by referring to it as profusive or rhizomatic, a confused and almost completely unregulated mishmash of the good and the bad. In addition, lax advertising regulations mean that companies are able to release advertisements claiming to cure atopic dermatitis in certain cases. It is not hard to imagine how new treatments, such as steroid withdrawal treatment, are able to spread quickly in this environment. In the UK, on the other hand, novel forms of alternative medicine are rare, and only relatively well-established kinds, such as homoeopathy, acupuncture, and yoga, have any noticeable presence. Advertising regulations are also extremely strict, such that producing false or misleading advertisements is next to impossible there. Promoting a treatment without a certain level of history and trustworthiness would therefore be a challenge.

Secondly, the significant differences in the structure of health care between Japan and the UK may be a factor in the success of steroid withdrawal treatment in Japan. In the UK, if NHS doctors provide treatment that does not follow official guidelines, they have a duty to explain why they have deviated from these guidelines. The type of treatment provided by modern medicine is standardized, and it is difficult for doctors to offer treatment such as steroid withdrawal treatment under their own judgement. In Japan, doctors are able to use their own discretion to some extent, and the fact that it is possible for them to ignore guidelines and offer steroid withdrawal treatment is a significant contrast.

When patients first fall sick in the UK, they must book an appointment with their local GP, and any consultation with a specialist dermatologist requires a referral from the GP. Even if steroid withdrawal doctors were to exist, patients would not be able to see them without such a referral, and furthermore, the general ability of patients to select their own doctors is limited. A referral system is used by part of the health care system in Japan, but, in most cases, patients are able to search for doctors who provide the treatment they desire and visit them directly. This system made it easier for patients to see steroid withdrawal doctors, and it is likely that patient reviews of treatment shared on the Internet and elsewhere helped the idea of steroid withdrawal spread.

As explained, Japan saw a trend toward steroid withdrawal, unlike in the UK; thus, it is important to discuss the consequences of this trend. In Japan, steroid withdrawal treatments were led mostly by the alternative medical market in the 1990s, but in the 2000s, these were mostly taken over by the steroid withdrawal treatment provided by steroid withdrawal doctors. The difficulty of discussing the value of steroid withdrawal treatments is that their treatments are a double-edged sword, both productive and exploitive. These treatments were productive in the sense that they reflected the patients' need to be freed from steroids and in the sense that they developed new methodologies of healing, which standard treatment could not implement. Most patients who stopped using steroids had realized that steroids could not control their symptoms anymore and that they needed to find a way to control them. After the withdrawal symptoms abated, most were happy that they no longer needed to depend on steroids. They thought that they would not have been able to maintain their relatively good condition if they had instead followed standard treatment. However, it was not always the case that patients could recover through steroid withdrawal treatments, and, in fact, some of patients had to sacrifice their social lives because of severe withdrawal symptoms that did not cease for more than ten years. Furthermore, some forms of alternative medicine could be very expensive and exploitive as profit-seeking services, though it is true that some services provided supportive care such as 24-hour telephone counselling. On the other hand, the steroid withdrawal treatment conducted by steroid withdrawal doctors was usually covered by health insurance and did not cost as much for patients. In this sense, the doctors' treatments may seem less exploitive. However, this is all complicated by the fact that neither standard treatment, nor alternative medicine, nor steroid withdrawal treatment was able to provide a cure to every patient, and, thus, there is no clear answer regarding which treatment was 'right' or 'wrong.'

In the end, it is important to consider what kinds of changes the patients who chose steroid withdrawal treatment could bring about by challenging standard treatment. There is the fact that patients' rejection of using steroids starting in the 1990s affected the attitudes of doctors who used to prescribe steroids in standard treatment. Some doctors, especially younger doctors, started to hesitate to use steroids. However, at the same time, the core members of the Japanese Dermatological Association began to insist on the need to educate not only patients but also doctors about the necessity of using steroids. Since the 2000s, this insistence has increased.

Thus, the patients' rejection of steroids has not changed mainstream medicine in a straightforward way; on the contrary, mainstream medicine has started promoting steroid treatment even more vigorously in an attempt to stop 'steroid-phobia.' Instead of changing mainstream medicine, then, steroid withdrawal treatments have continued to be provided outside the mainstream in order to meet patients' needs.

Making a comparison with the UK in this way suggests that the situation in Japan is not necessarily present in other countries and that particular circumstances fostered the patient knowledge that has encouraged defiance against standard treatment. The nature of this patient knowledge in Japan will be considered in more detail.

## Scientific evidence and patient knowledge

### Self-help groups in the 1990s

In Japan, in the early 1990s, the debate around topical steroids reached its peak. Key parties included doctors backing standard treatment, steroid withdrawal doctors, alternative medicine practitioners, patient self-help groups, and the media. Opinions were split across the different sectors on the point of whether or not topical steroids were safe, and public opinion was leaning increasingly towards the idea that they were dangerous. Special reports and films were being produced around this time on the topic of atopic dermatitis or topical steroids, including the documentary *Kimyō na Dekigoto Atopy (The Odd Phenomenon of Atopy)* in 1991, the special report about steroids on a news channel titled *'Mahō' no Kusuri Steroid-zai no Otoshiana (The Trap of the 'Magical' Medicine of Steroids)* in 1992 which is covered in Chapter 1, and the Nihon TV documentary titled *Shinobiyoru Yakugai!? – Kyūzō' suru Atopy Jyūshōsha (Hidden Side Effects!? – Patients with Serious Cases of Atopy Spiking)* in 1997. What all of these productions shared in common was the portrayal of all atopic dermatitis patients as victims, suffering from the side effects of steroids. The alternative medicine industry took advantage of this trend to criticize the steroid treatment carried out at conventional hospitals, and, in turn, increase its own profits, expanding to such an extent that it led to what was mockingly referred to as the Atopy Business. Patients also began complaining to their doctors that they did not want to use steroids, and steroid withdrawal doctors emerged as dermatologists tried to sympathize with these patients.

Building on this momentum, several self-help groups began to become increasingly political in the 1990s. For example, the self-help group Atopy Steroid Jyōhō Centre (Atopy Steroid Information Centre), which was based in Osaka, aimed to revolutionize health care at the time. The group summarized their aims this way:

> When continually using steroid medication to treat atopic dermatitis, there are people who eventually see that steroids are no longer able to treat their atopic dermatitis, and there are even people who have to endure suffering beyond that of atopic dermatitis as a result. We have started to give a voice to people who do not want to use steroids for their atopic dermatitis. Preventing yet more people from suffering the pain of discontinuing steroids after a lengthy fight against atopic dermatitis is one of the main goals of the Information Centre.
>
> (Atopy Steroid Information Centre, 1999)

As can be inferred from the group's aims, it continued to work to bring attention to the suffering caused by steroids and to bring about change in the health care system. The group's activities were diverse. One of the group's representatives, Junko Sumiyoshi, published a book in 1996, titled *Steroid wo Yameta*

*Riyū – Ridatsu Taikensha 35 nin ni yoru Shōgen (Why I Quit Steroids – The Experiences of 35 People)*, which gave 35 accounts of people who had stopped using steroids and had experienced a relapse (Sumiyoshi, 1996). In 1999, the group also carried out a detailed survey of 1,558 atopic dermatitis patients in order to learn more about the disease, steroid treatment, informed consent, withdrawal from society, and so on. The results showed that half of the patients had been using topical steroids for over five years, 76% had experienced side effects, and 95% were now against using steroids (Atopy Steroid Information Centre, 1999). Based on these results, the group submitted a petition to the Ministry of Health and Welfare with the following request:

> Since the number of patients having used steroids from five to ten years is high, we would like to see criteria for long-term use that avoids side effects, treatment guidelines for side effects, and controlled studies of long-term topical steroid use.
>
> (*Mainichi Shimbun*, 28 June 1998)

The group's activities were also covered by newspapers, and it is fair to say that they garnered a reasonable level of attention.

During this time, other groups were also engaged in political activism. For example, one of the people I interviewed, Junya, was active as a member of Steroid Hifushō wo Kangaeru Kai (the Steroid-Induced Skin Condition Group). The group actively contacted politicians to demand recognition of the harm caused by steroids, and they requested that the Pharmaceuticals and Medical Devices Agency recognize the relapses associated with steroids as qualifying for payment of medical expenses or disability pension. While these efforts ultimately had little success, it was significant in the 1990s that self-help groups showed a resolve to effect change in the health care system.

Chapter 1 illustrated through the research of Hilary Arksey, Steven Epstein, and Takuya Matsushige that in order for patient knowledge to influence the formation of medical knowledge, patients must either work together with experts or acquire a level of professional knowledge that allows them to debate on the scientific level. The MMR vaccine debate introduced by Matsushige further suggests that the opinions of amateurs are typically seen as unscientific and therefore dismissed by experts.

In fact, the string of activism by atopic dermatitis self-help groups in the 1990s reached a very similar conclusion to those in the MMR debate in the UK. The following two aspects of the MMR debate are pertinent, and they also apply in the case of atopic dermatitis. The first aspect is that everyone involved in the debate was in a realm of uncertainty (Matsushige, 2010). In other words, although there was no evidence for a cause-and-effect relationship between MMR and autism, there was also no definitive evidence to refute the theory that MMR caused autism, which meant that neither side was able to use evidence to sway the debate. This is also true in the case of atopic dermatitis, since there is no solid evidence that the long-term use of topical steroids is safe, nor is there any evidence to suggest that steroids should not be used over the long term.

The second pertinent aspect of the debate is that, despite the lack of evidence for either argument, the claims of the non-professional side were dismissed as unscientific, and the opinions of the experts prevailed. From the perspective of health officials and doctors, non-professional judgement is dangerous and the situation needs to be handled as a case of debunking lies (Matsushige, 2010).

Similarly, in the case of atopic dermatitis, the premise is that the opinions of patients are unscientific. Furthermore, the opinion of patients that steroids are dangerous is not to be investigated for its validity, but is to be seen as a lie that should be extinguished. This view led to the creation of standard treatment guidelines in order to spread 'correct' information. Several versions of the guidelines were produced between the 1990s and the 2000s. All of them state that topical steroids are safe when used correctly, and they clearly recommend their use as the basis of all treatment. From the 1990s, the guidelines were determined by the Japanese Dermatological Association. These again stressed the legitimacy of topical steroids, which also led public opinion in the same direction. The way the situation was handled at the time was not to investigate the merits of topical steroids scientifically, but rather to attempt to stress the legitimacy of their position through the naming choice of 'standard treatment,' the establishment of guidelines, and the involvement of major media outlets, such as the *Asahi Shimbun*, the *Yomiuri Shimbun*, and Japan's largest broadcasting corporation, *NHK*.

When average people actually judge what is legitimate or fair, they rarely rely on scientific evidence or data to make their decision. They are greatly influenced instead by what is considered legitimate and may believe that what their doctor says is correct, that following everybody else is likely safe, that the Japanese Dermatological Association must be correct, and so on. Similar opinions were frequently apparent during the interviews carried out for this book.

> There are people who just think you should rely on the hospital. It's really hard to get your partner to understand when you try steroid withdrawal. They do take it seriously, but they really just want you to go to the hospital. They might ask you to go to a symposium introducing a new drug or something, since some people just can't get away from the idea of drugs, clinics, and hospitals. ... There are so many people who are too stubborn to understand the suffering involved with steroid withdrawal. They think that it's better just to rub in the steroids – that a doctor would never suggest such a terrible treatment. Depending on the person, they might even think I'm possessed or brainwashed like part of some kind of cult.
>
> (Asami, 28, female)

Asami's partner put a lot of trust in hospitals and doctors and was of the view that the topical steroids they prescribed could never be harmful. Akio described his father's views similarly.

> It was so hard to get my father to understand back then. From his point of view, the Japanese Dermatological Association was probably right. His view was that steroids had a history, and there was no way they were bad or poisonous. So, he thought I should follow the mainstream opinion, and we argued about that a lot back then.
>
> (Akio, 31, male)

Akio's father thus also appeared to trust the Japanese Dermatological Association and the mainstream opinion that topical steroids were safe. In this way, the claims of legitimacy brought about by the establishment of guidelines had a great impact on what people thought. As a result, it appears that standard treatment successfully gained legitimacy in 2005, as quotes like the following suggest:

> It appears that the establishment of the guidelines has begun to bring an end to the chaos seen at clinics and hospitals.
>
> (Nakagawa, 2005: 1)

My own investigation showed that of 30 Japanese people who attempted steroid withdrawal treatment in the 1980s and 1990s, seven had resumed topical steroid treatment by the 2000s. It is likely that their choice to resume this treatment was influenced by the attained legitimacy of standard treatment, and by the public opinion that topical steroids were safe.

As a result of the establishment of guidelines by standard treatment advocates and other campaigns, self-help groups like the Atopy Steroid Information Centre and the Steroid-Induced Skin Condition Group eventually discontinued their activities. Junya, who was active as a member of the latter group, spoke of the declining motivation among the group during his interview:

> I wanted to spread the word that people were being harmed, but the world is so big, and I started to feel what a challenge it was more and more. I lost my enthusiasm for it, and my motivation, too. I guess it doesn't really bother me that people don't care about it so much anymore. But I want the health care system to recognize that I'm in this state because of steroids. I want people to know that it's because of these things that I can't work.
>
> (Junya, 39, male)

The efforts of patients in the 1990s to bring about changes in health care were thus significantly set back, but the activities of atopic dermatitis patients did not completely end there. It is useful to examine the direction patients took after these setbacks. Atopy-free.com and Atopicco Network for Children of the Earth, for instance, took completely different approaches in looking for ways to develop patient knowledge, and they serve as interesting examples when considering this knowledge.

## The self-help group Atopy-free.com

In trying to bring about change in the health care system, the self-help group Atopy-free.com continues the approach of the Atopy Steroid Information Centre. In fact, Atopy-free.com was born partly as a way of bringing together readers of the newsletter *Yū Net*, which was produced by Junko Sumiyoshi, one of the founders of the Atopy Steroid Information Centre, and Sumiyoshi is listed as one of the staff members of Atopy-free.com also.

When the group was founded in 2005, Naoko Andō, one of its founders, was guiding it in a similar direction to that of the Atopy Steroid Information Centre. Naoko has herself experienced steroid withdrawal, which she credits with improving her symptoms, and is also a scientist specializing in food toxicology. She currently works as a professor in the department of applied chemistry at Tōyō University. In line with her background, Naoko thinks as a scientist and advances the debate at the scientific level in an attempt to earn the trust of the medical establishment. In 2006, she received a research grant from The Takagi Fund for Citizen Science to carry out a survey of 1,000 atopic dermatitis patients who had moved away from standard treatment, and she published the results in 2008 as a book titled *Atopīseihifuen Kanjya 1000 nin no Shōgen* (*The Voices of 1,000 Atopic Dermatitis Patients*). The book highlights the lack of evidence showing that long-term use of topical steroids is safe and emphasizes the need for investigation into their side effects. It also demonstrates with quantitative data the existence of the topical steroid relapse, the variety of patient struggles at clinics and hospitals, and the types of suffering they endure in their social lives and at home (Andō, 2008). This study shows similarities with one conducted by Atopy Steroid Information Centre in 1999, and both used quantitative data to argue on a scientific level with the aim of gaining medical legitimacy.

This aspiration for medical legitimacy is also common among steroid withdrawal doctors, who are closely involved with Atopy-free.com. One such doctor, Shigeki Fujisawa (2012), has released data showing that steroid withdrawal treatment is more effective than steroid treatment and continues to work to have its effectiveness recognized. Dr. Fujisawa released the treatment success rate of his patients aged between 0 and 17 years. The participants comprised 434 patients who had never used topical steroids and 290 patients who had experience using topical steroids. Both groups of patients were guided through steroid withdrawal treatment, and their success rates were compared. The results showed that patients who had never used topical steroids were able to see improvements faster than those who had (Fujisawa, 2012). Dr. Fujisawa (2012: 160) said the following of his findings:

> There is an inconsistency in the idea that using corticosteroids properly will not lead to side effects. What this data shows is that corticosteroid treatment contributes to the severity and chronicity of atopic dermatitis. Although this was a case-control study, it supports the idea that not providing corticosteroid treatment makes it easier to recover from atopic dermatitis.

What both Naoko and Dr. Fujisawa aim to do is to point out that problems exist with steroid treatment even though it is positioned as legitimate, and to have steroid withdrawal treatment recognized as an alternative form of legitimate treatment. Furthermore, it seems apparent that in order to achieve their aim, they are attempting to fight in terms of scientific validity by presenting data that show the superior efficacy of steroid withdrawal treatment.

As discussed in the first chapter, for patients to be involved in the formation of medical knowledge, they must either work with experts or be able to debate at an expert level. The goals that science and medical experts such as Naoko and Dr. Fujisawa aim to achieve seem like prime examples of this. Efforts such as these to gain medical legitimacy on a scientific level could be seen as patient knowledge that is attempting to advance into the realm of professional knowledge.[1]

What cannot be overlooked, however, is that patient knowledge encompasses more than just a scientific aspect. As mentioned in Chapter 5, within the self-help group Atopy-free.com, there was some discrepancy evident between the goals of experts like Naoko and Dr. Fujisawa and the interests of the non-professional patient members. What this means is that the interests of patients are not exclusively focused on experts attempting to gain medical legitimacy, but also on things such as food, work, and talking to peers. The latter set of interests has no relation to the scientific or medical debate and could be seen as connected instead to local or living knowledge. Regarding this knowledge, issues such as bringing about change in health care and spreading awareness about the harm caused by steroids are subordinated, as the focus shifts to more familiar problems such as how to get the most out of life or how to retain a job. For this reason, Atopy-free.com is an amalgam of the two viewpoints: experts aiming to gain medical legitimacy and patients interested in more familiar issues.

### The self-help group and authorized NPO Atopicco Network for Children of the Earth

The aims of Atopicco Network for Children of the Earth seem more oriented to local or living knowledge than scientific knowledge. At the very least, it is not the group's approach to become involved with expert medical knowledge related to spreading awareness about the harm caused by steroids or about the effectiveness of steroid withdrawal treatment. For example, the group organizes a summer camp for children suffering from allergies and atopy to help educate them about the environment. The camp is held just outside of Tokyo, where children are able to spend two nights and three days among nature with their parents. The 2012 brochure promotes the camp this way:

> Come and eat delicious food, play, experience the delights of nature, and make time to reflect on everyday life and parent-child relationships. Whether you're the same as others or different, would you like to experience a place where everyone accepts each other for who they are?
>
> (Atopicco Network for Children of the Earth, 2013)

It is clear from this that the camp includes many themes that are closely related to everyday life, including food, fun, family, reflection, and acceptance of differences. These wide-ranging themes are subtly included in the programme of the camp. As an example of the themes of food and relationships, the group asks each child in advance if they have any food allergies and makes an effort to provide food that allows everyone to eat the same thing. For example, the dinner at the 2006 camp did not use ingredients such as soy, wheat, or eggs. Allergens were completely removed by using clever replacements: the miso soup used chestnut miso instead of regular miso and rice-based soy sauce for flavouring, and the simmered meat and potatoes (*nikujaga*) used dried tapioca noodles and Japanese basil (*shiso*) oil.

If every child suffering from allergies had brought their own lunchbox, a lot of effort could have been saved in preparing the meals, so this raises the question of why the group was so particular about having everyone eat the same food. The reason is that for children who usually cannot eat the same food as everyone else due to allergies and thus find themselves alienated from others when taking their own lunchbox, being able to eat the same food as everyone else is a precious experience, and this is something the group wants to facilitate. As Arthur Kleinman points out, the experience of the patient is not simply an issue of disease, but rather something that should be seen as an issue of an illness that also encompasses society, culture, and human relationships. Illnesses such as allergies and atopic dermatitis do not simply create the problem of symptoms, but also lead to problems that affect human relationships, such as children being alienated because they cannot eat the same food as others. By encouraging reflection on the various factors that surround illness, including food, the environment, and human relationships, the group aims to help people find a way to live alongside their illness. It thus appears evident that what the group is aiming for is primarily local or living knowledge.

The direction of the group is fundamentally different from patient knowledge concerned with medical legitimacy, which is premised on the idea that 'correct knowledge' exists. While in that model patients and experts shape their arguments around this shared premise, Atopicco Network for Children of the Earth does not fight for legitimacy, but rather appears to aim to diversify the values of its members. Even in regard to medical legitimacy, the values of patients are respected regardless of whether they choose to use topical steroids or not. At first glance, then, it may appear that the group has no desire to change the current situation, but when looking more closely at their activities, one finds that they are merely not concerned with gaining legitimacy in the limited field of medical knowledge. The group's activities instead tackle a relatively wide range of problems, including surveys related to food allergies, collaborating to establish asthma guidelines, and investigating the relationship between environmental pollution and asthma. The group also carries out telephone consultations and offers advice on topics including building relationships, approaching doctors, negotiating, and getting people to understand. This suggests that the group actually does seek some level of change, though primarily in the context of the individual.

The form of knowledge seen here differs from that pursued by the likes of Arksey and Epstein, as it does not come into direct contact with medical or professional knowledge. As a result, in any debate concerning medical legitimacy, it is likely that this knowledge would simply be brushed aside. However, there is a difference between the knowledge pursued by experts and the knowledge desired by patients. No matter how many debates concerning medical legitimacy are won by those with professional knowledge, when looking at everyday life through the eyes of a patient, it is doubtful that professional knowledge is of any practical use. It is therefore vital to consider knowledge from the perspective of the patient.

## Scientific evidence and the context of the individual

Currently, the best criterion for judging the legitimacy of medical knowledge is scientific evidence. However, for individual patients in real life, scientific evidence is not necessarily the only criterion. When looking at the reasons the patients interviewed for this book decided to stop using topical steroids, there are many cases in which personal experience strongly influenced their decision.

> My body felt terrible, and it became harder and harder to tell whether I'd be better off with or without steroids. So, when I tried quitting them for a while as a test, my skin did become dry and rough, but my body felt better overall. When I was using steroids, I felt like I was often tired to the core of my body, so compared to that, I started thinking I was better off not using steroids.
>
> (Ryōhei, 34, male)

> The reason I stopped using steroids in my second year of middle school was because I felt they'd stopped working for me.
>
> (Yukie, 39, female)

> When I was using steroids, my skin was festering. It would fester where the steroids were suppressing my immune system, so I had to rub in antibiotics. I'd rub in steroids and then antibiotics. That doctor told me to continue doing it, but nothing changed even after two or three years. He just said the festering was because the steroids were suppressing my immune system. It was a vicious cycle that I wanted to break, so I changed hospitals. I was switched to pine tar ointment and got off of steroids.
>
> (Saki, 46, female)

For people who speak of experiences such as 'my body felt terrible,' 'they'd stopped working,' and 'my skin was festering,' topical steroids are seen as something negative regardless of the amount of scientific evidence that may or may not exist showing that using them long term is safe. Patients' judgements are based instead on their personal interest in how something will affect them specifically.

Looking at the overall percentages, it is likely that the number of patients who experience festering skin is actually low, but for Saki, as long as her own skin is festering, she will no doubt feel like avoiding topical steroids.

Scientific evidence provides a general representation of a given sample. For experts, this is valuable data, but for individual patients, their interest is inevitably focused on how it affects them personally. Matsushige (2010: 141) raises concerns about how the focus of medicine on such evidence leads to diseases being reduced to one-dimensional ideas:

> 'Evidence' derived from statistical 'significance' is nothing more than the product of a world supposed from an average sample. In reality, patients live in numerous and diverse worlds that deviate from the average. Once the one-dimensional approach of interpreting reality that makes up the statistical method at the foundation of medicine is given the overwhelming power that 'evidence' provides, diseases are interpreted simply in terms of medicine, and not as the aggregation of society, culture, psychology and so on that they are. The result is that any path back to the original context of the generalized knowledge is cut off.

The problem presented here is that generalized knowledge presented as evidence cannot be applied to the individual context for effective use. This has also long been an issue within evidence-based medicine and narrative-based medicine. Evidence-based medicine is often simply associated with the idea of pursuing a scientific foundation through randomized trials, but it was originally defined as the process of choosing the optimal treatment for an individual patient after considering that patient's particular situation and values. However, choosing the optimal treatment for an individual patient—taking the specific circumstances of that patient into account—is a significant challenge in reality. One of the advocates of narrative-based medicine, Tricia Greenhalgh, was originally a pioneer of evidence-based medicine. However, she began to fear that the single-minded focus on finding scientific foundations was leading to the loss of the individual patient's perspective, and she went on to propose the idea of narrative-based medicine (Tsujiuchi et al., 2009). Narrative-based medicine is the concept of drawing attention to the need to listen to individual patient's stories, and it could be seen as a method of taking the individual needs of patients into account. Nevertheless, even with the concept of narrative-based medicine, it is still a challenge to connect the generalized knowledge that constitutes 'evidence' with the individuality that narratives represent. Ultimately, in the formation of medical knowledge, the generalized knowledge of scientific evidence is prized, whereas individual patients value the individuality inherent in the question of whether a given treatment is effective for them specifically. For health care workers, to what degree that individuality should be taken into account remains a significant question.

In carrying out research on patient-centred medicine, Matsushige concluded that there are two main ways that health care workers have attempted to handle patient individuality. First, drawing on evidence-based medicine, is evidence-based patient choice, a model in which patients make informed choices after understanding the available evidence. Evidence-based patient choice follows the philosophy of evidence-based medicine, and it involves providing medical information to patients while communicating the level of validity this information has as evidence. The philosophy of evidence-based patient choice is to have patients then choose their own treatment based on the evidence presented (Matsushige, 2010).

Second is patient partnership, a model in which health care workers build a partnership with patients. A key characteristic of this approach is the way patients are given an equal footing with doctors in treatment settings. Decision-making regarding treatment is therefore determined by the opinions of both doctors and patients (Matsushige, 2010).

Matsushige points out that although both approaches achieve the same goal of providing patient-centred medicine, they differ in their respective aims. With evidence-based patient choice, the focus when choosing treatment is on both the doctor and patient sharing scientific evidence, but in the case of patient partnership, the doctor and patient are each expected to bring their own judgement criteria. In this way, patient partnership allows for the discussion of factors outside the category of health care, including patient preferences, culture, and faith.

Even in patient-centred medicine, the process involved in deciding treatment may well differ, depending on whether the scope of the patient's choice is limited to the level of scientific evidence or if it includes factors relating to local or living knowledge that at first appear unrelated to medicine, such as preferences, faith, or economic conditions. The dilemma of applying the generalized knowledge of evidence to individual patients is also closely connected to how deeply the patient's individual needs can be taken into account and to the scope that they are afforded.

## The issues raised by atopic dermatitis

In the introduction to this book, the case of Asami raised the following question. Was her decision to suffer through a terrible relapse an unscientific action or the choice of a patient that should be respected? Thinking purely in terms of the professional knowledge of doctors, guidelines, and scientific evidence drawn from statistics, Asami's actions seem unscientific. The knowledge shared among doctors does not include the fears of patients regarding the risks of long-term topical steroid use, such as that topical steroids might lose their efficacy after ten years or that they cause relapses; these fears are dismissed out of hand as unscientific superstitions. On the other hand, if patient opinions regarding topical steroids were truly respected, Asami's decision would be seen as a respected patient choice, and she could expect appropriate support.

Where would Asami's choice currently fit in Japan between an unscientific act and a respected patient choice? In other words, to what extent does Japanese health care really respect the opinions of patients? The answer seems clear: in the mainstream practice of standard treatment or modern medicine, the actions of patients like Asami are seen as unscientific, and the commonly accepted approach is to attempt to convince such patients to return to standard treatment based on guidelines or medical textbooks. However, as a kind of sanctuary for patients who cannot accept this approach in Japan, steroid withdrawal doctors and alternative medicine provide forms of treatment that do respect the opinions of patients. In other words, while mainstream treatment as a whole is not adapted to the individual, other forms of treatment take patients' needs into account. There is no sign of mainstream treatment moving towards respecting patients' opinions, but there are at least efforts in Japan to bring about change in mainstream treatment, primarily by steroid withdrawal doctors and self-help groups, and that is one of the bigger differences between Japan and the UK.

In the treatment of atopic dermatitis, then, what would happen if standard treatment's approach was not to convince reluctant patients to use steroids, but to provide treatment in accordance with the patient's opinion? Two issues arise in this scenario.

First, even if patients insist that they do not want to use topical steroids, under current standard treatment, there are no alternative forms of treatment anyway, so the choice is moot. The common premise among evidence-based medicine, narrative-based medicine, and patient-centred medicine is that the treatment desired by the patient exists among the choices available to the doctor, and the idea that the doctor would not be able to provide what the patient requests is never considered. What becomes evident from atopic dermatitis case studies is that in order for patients' opinions to be respected, doctors need to provide treatment that they have yet to offer.

Second is the possibility of doctors interpreting patient knowledge as a meaningful form of information. The disconnect between doctors and patients surrounding the risks of topical steroids could be a result of the lack of clarity regarding the long-term risks of topical steroids. A mere 60 years have passed since the use of topical steroids was approved, and the only means of assessing the impact of using steroids over an entire lifetime is to look at the condition of patients alive today. In this sense, those in possession of the data regarding the long-term side effects are not doctors, but patients. One of the biggest problems today is that despite the fact that the experience of patients is vital for discovering long-term side effects, the doctors responsible for creating medical knowledge dismiss patient experiential knowledge as misperception and unscientific. The challenge is that the real-life experiences of patients, such as seeing topical steroids lose their effectiveness over time, do not easily translate into change or transform professional knowledge. As the MMR vaccine debate, RSI, and AIDS activism have shown, the chances of effecting change in professional or medical knowledge are greatly increased with knowledge backed by science. To be effective would require finding a means of converting the real-life experiences of patients into convincing scientific data. This overlaps with the efforts of patient and scientist Naoko Andō, for example, who attempted to achieve this by quantifying patient experiences after conducting surveys.

Health care workers would also need to show a greater willingness to take the real-life experiences of patients seriously. Doctors can evaluate scientific evidence that is presented clearly as numerical data, but it is clearly more difficult to consider how they should interpret the unquantified narratives and experiences of patients. For example, the steroid withdrawal doctors Shigeki Fujisawa, Mototsugu Fukaya, and Marvin J. Rapaport are attempting to bring their arguments into the medical debate by quantifying the course of treatment of the patients they have seen, and they have authored studies and books. This could also be seen as an effort to convert patient experiences into scientific knowledge. But the influence these efforts will have on health care in the future remains to be seen.

## Note

1 However, though it is necessary to take this approach to win credibility among experts, it is important to note that it is done mainly by those people who are already in a position close to that of experts, such as patients with a scientific background or steroid withdrawal doctors.

## References

Andō, N. 2008, *Atopīseihifuen Kanjya 1000 nin no Shōgen (Testimony from 1000 atopic dermatitis patients)*, Tokyo: Kodomo no Miraisha.

Atopicco Network for Children of the Earth. 2013, *Natsuyasumi Kankyō Kyōiku Camp (Environment education camp in summer vacation)*, viewed 21 March 2019, www.atopicco.org/activity/education/.

Atopy/Steroid Information Centre. 1999, *Atopy/steroid ni Kansuru Ankēto Chōsa: Chōsa Hōkokusho (Questionnaire on atopy/steroids: a report)*, Osaka: Atopy/Steroid Information Centre.

Fujisawa, S. 2012, "'Datsu steroid' toha: sono honshitsu ha (What is steroid withdrawal: its essence)", In Kamide, R. (ed.) *Takumi ni Manabu Hifuka Gaiyō Ryōhō: Furuki wo Ikasu, Saishin wo Tsukau (Topical dermatologic therapy learning from masters: making use of old technique, using new technique)*, Tokyo: Zen Nihon Byōin Syuppankai, pp. 157–162.

Kleinman, A. 1988, *The illness narratives: suffering, healing, and the human condition*, New York: Basic Books.

Matsushige, T. 2010, *Kanjya Chūshin no Iryō toiu Gensetsu: Kanjya no 'Chi' no Shakaigaku (The theory of 'patient-centered medicine': sociology of patient 'knowledge')*, Tokyo: Rikkyo University Press.

Nakagawa, H. 2005, "Atopīseihifuen chiryō no mokuteki toha nanika (What is the purpose of atopic dermatitis treatment?)", In Nakagawa, H. (ed.) *Atopīseihifuen Chiryō no Jissai: Protopic-Nankō Shiyōhō wo Fukumete (The reality of atopic dermatitis treatment: including the usage of protopic ointment)*, Tokyo: Shindan to Chiryōsha, pp.1–8.

Sumiyoshi, J. 1996, *Steroid wo Yameta Riyū: Ridatsu Keikensha 35 nin ni yoru Shōgen (Reasons for stopping steroids: testimony from 35 patients)*, Tokyo: Tsuge Shobō Shinsha.

Tsujiuchi, T. 2004, "Post-modern iryō ni okeru modern: hokan daitai iryō no jissen to senmonshokuka (Modern in post-modern medicine: practice and professionalization of complementary and alternative medicine)", In Kondo, H. & Ukigaya, S. (eds.) *Gendai Iryō no Minzokushi (An ethnography of contemporary medicine)*, Tokyo: Akashi Shoten, pp. 183–224.

Tsujiuchi, T., Nakagami, A. & Taniguchi, R. 2009, "Iryō jinruigaku kara mita hokan daitai iryō no sekai" (A medical anthropological perspective of the world of complementary and alternative medicine), *Byōin (Hospital)*, vol. 68, no. 11, pp. 919–923.

# Bibliography

Akagi, T. 2005, *Allergy to Tanoshiku Ikiru* (*Living in harmony with allergy*), Tokyo: Gendai Shokan.

Akagi, T. 2006, *Atopīseihifuen no Taiken wo Kataru: Otona ni natta Kanjya tachi* (*Reliving atopic dermatitis: from patients who are now adults*), Tokyo: NPO Atopicco Network for Children of the Earth.

Andō, N. 2008, *Atopīseihifuen Kanjya 1000 nin no Shōgen* (*Testimony from 1000 atopic dermatitis patients*), Tokyo: Kodomo no Miraisha.

Arai, M. 1994, *Kōkoku no Shakaikeizaishi* (*The socio-economic history of advertisement*), Tokyo: Tōyō Keizai Shinpōsha.

Arksey, H. 1998, *RSI and the experts: the construction of medical knowledge*, London: UCL Press.

Atopicco Network for Children of the Earth. 2012, *Atopicco Chikyū no Ko Network ga Mezasu Mono* (*The goal of atopicco network for children of the earth*), viewed 21 March 2019, www.atopicco.org/philosophy.html.

Atopicco Network for Children of the Earth. 2013, *Natsuyasumi Kankyō Kyōiku Camp* (*Environment education camp in summer vacation*), viewed 21 March 2019, www.atopicco.org/activity/education/.

Atopy/Steroid Information Centre. 1999, *Atopy/steroid ni Kansuru Ankēto Chōsa: Chōsa Hōkokusho* (*Questionnaire on atopy/steroids: a report*), Osaka: Atopy/Steroid Information Centre.

Brown, P. 2007, *Toxic exposures: contested illnesses and the environmental health movement*, New York: Columbia University Press.

Brown, P., Morello-Frosch R. & Zavestoski, S. 2011, *Contested illnesses: citizens, science, and health social movements*, Berkeley: University of California Press.

Callon, M. & Rabeharisoa, V. 2003, "Research "in the wild" and the shaping of new social identities", *Technology in Society*, vol. 25, no. 2, pp. 193–204.

Cant, S. & Sharma, U. 1999, *A new medical pluralism?: alternative medicine, doctors, patients and the state*, London: UCL Press.

Charman, C. R., Morris, A. D. & Williams, H. C. 2000, "Topical corticosteroid phobia in patients with atopic eczema", *British Journal of Dermatology*, vol. 142, no. 5, pp. 931–936.

Crossley, N. 2006, *Contesting psychiatry: social movements in mental health*, London: Routledge.

Department of Health. 2001, *The expert patient: a new approach to chronic disease management for the 21st century*, London: Crown Copyright.

Epstein, S. 1996, *Impure science: AIDS, activism, and the politics of knowledge*, Berkeley: University of California Press.

Ezaki, H. 1988, *Kao Tsuburetemo Kagayaite: Steroid Nankōka Soshō 6-nen no Kiroku* (*Keep shining even if your face is ruined: six years of steroid ointment litigation*), Tokyo: Ikkōsha.

Fowler, A. 2010, "A life less ordinary: Angeline Fowler describes how lifelong eczema has shaped her life", *Exchange*, no. 137, pp. 12–14.

Freidson, E. 1970, *Professional dominance: the social structure of medical care*, 1st ed., New Brunswick: Aldine; Atherton Press.

Fujisawa, S. 2004, *Atopī Chiryō Kakumei* (*The revolution of treatment of atopic dermatitis*), Tokyo: Nagaoka Shoten.

Fujisawa, S. 2012, "'Datsu steroid' toha: sono honshitsu ha (What is steroid withdrawal: its essence)", In Kamide, R. (ed.) *Takumi ni Manabu Hifuka Gaiyō Ryōhō: Furuki wo Ikasu, Saishin wo Tsukau* (*Topical dermatologic therapy learning from masters: making use of old technique, using new technique*), Tokyo: Zen Nihon Byōin Syuppankai, pp. 157–162.

Fukaya, M. 1999, *Steroid Izon: Steroid wo Yametai Atopīseihifuen Kanjya no Tameni* (*Steroid addiction: for patients who want to stop using steroids*), Tokyo: Tsuge Shobō Shinsha.

Fukaya, M. 2010, *Steroid Izon 2010: Nihon Hifukagakkai wa Atopīseihifuen Shinryō Guideline wo Syūsei Seyo* (*Steroid Addiction 2010: Alter the Guideline of Atopic Dermatitis by Japanese Dermatological Association*), Tokyo: Iyaku Bijiransu Center.

Fukaya, M., Satō, K., Satō, M., Kimata, H., Fujisawa, S., Dozono, H., Yoshizawa, J. & Minaguchi, S. 2014, "Topical steroid addiction in atopic dermatitis", *Drug, Healthcare and Patient Safety*, vol. 6, pp. 131–138.

Fuller, R. C. 1989, *Alternative medicine and American religious life*, Oxford: Oxford University Press.

Furue, M., Saeki, H., Furukawa, F., Hide, M., Ohtsuki, M., Katayama, I., Sasaki, R., Sudō, H. & Takehara, K. 2009, "Atopīseihifuen shinryō guideline (Guidelines for Atopic Dermatitis Treatment)", In *Nihon Hifuka Gakkaishi* (*The Japanese Journal of Dermatology*), vol. 119, no. 8, pp. 1515–1534.

Furue, M., Terao, H., Rikihisa, W., Urabe, K., Kinukawa, N., Nose, Y. & Koga, T. 2003, "Clinical dose and adverse effects of topical steroids in daily management of atopic dermatitis", *British Journal of Dermatology*, vol. 148, no. 1, pp. 128–133.

Gennep, A. V. 2004, *The rites of passage*, London: Routledge.

Good, B. 1994, *Medicine, rationality, and experience: an anthropological perspective*, Cambridge: Cambridge University Press.

Greenhalgh, T. & Hurwitz, B. 1998, *Narrative based medicine: dialogue and discourse in clinical practice*, London: BMJ.

Hajar, T., Leshem, Y. A., Hanifin, J. M., Nedorost, S. T., Lio, P. A., Paller, A. S., Block, J. & Simpson, E. L. 2015, "A systematic review of topical corticosteroid withdrawal ("steroid addiction") in patients with atopic dermatitis and other dermatoses", *Journal of the American Academy of Dermatology*, vol. 72, no. 3, pp. 541–549.e2.

Hess, D. J. 1999, *Evaluating alternative cancer therapies: a guide to the science and politics of an emerging medical field*, New Brunswick: Rutgers University Press.

Hoare, C., Po, A. L. & Williams, H. U. 2000, "Systematic review of treatments for atopic eczema", *Health Technology Assessment*, vol. 4, no. 37, pp. 1–191.

Ikeda, M. 1995, "Hi-seiyō iryō (Non-western medicine)," In Kuroda, K. (ed.) *Gendai Iryō no Shakaigaku* (*Sociology of modern medicine*), Kyoto: Sekai Shisōsha, pp. 202–224.

Janzen, J. M. 1978, *The quest for therapy in Lower Zaire*, Berkeley: University of California Press.

Japan Allergy Tomono Kai. 2010, *Kanjya dakara Wakaru Atopīseihifuen: Soboku na Gimon kara Chiryōhō made (Atopic dermatitis, which patients can understand: from simple questions to the ways of treatment)*, Tokyo: Shōgakukan.

Jordan, S. 2003, *A members' guide to the management of atopic eczema*, London: National Eczema Society.

Kanamaru, H. 1996, *Atopī ni Katsu Network (Network for overcoming atopy)*, Tokyo: Kōsaidō Shuppan.

Katō, N., Saeki, H., Nakahara, T., Tanaka, A., Kabashima, K., Sugaya M., Murota, H., Ebihara, T., Kataoka, Y., Aihara, M. & Etō, T. 2016, "Atopīseihifuen guideline (Guidelines for atopic dermatitis treatment)", *Nihon Hifuka Gakkaishi (The Japanese Journal of Dermatology)*, vol. 126, no. 2, pp. 121–155.

Kay, J., Gawkrodger, D. J., Mortimer, M. J. & Jaron, A. G. 1994, "The prevalence of childhood atopic eczema in a general population", *Journal of the American Academy of Dermatology*, vol. 30, no. 1, pp. 35–39.

Klawiter, M. 2008, *The biopolitics of breast cancer: changing cultures of disease and activism*, Minneapolis: University of Minnesota Press.

Kleinman, A. 1981, *Patients and healers in the context of culture: an exploration of the borderland between anthropology, medicine, and psychiatry*, Berkeley: University of California Press.

Kleinman, A. 1988, *The illness narratives: suffering, healing, and the human condition*, New York: Basic Books.

Kodama, Y. 1998, *'Byōki' no Tanjyō: Kindai Iryō no Kigen (Birth of 'disease': the origin of modern medicine)*, Tokyo: Heibonsha.

Kuroda, K. 2000, "Minkan iryō to seitō iryō no chiseigakuteki 'kankei' (The geopolitical 'relationship' between folk medicine and orthodox medicine)", In Satō, J. (ed.) *Bunka Genshō toshite no Iyashi: Minkan Iryō no Genzai (Healing as a cultural phenomenon: the current status of folk medicine)*, Osaka: Medicus Shuppan, pp. 143–184.

Larsen, F. S., & Hanifin, J. M. 1992, "Secular change in the occurrence of atopic dermatitis", *Acta dermato-venereologica. Supplementum*, vol. 176, pp. 7–12.

Latour, B. 1987, *Science in action: how to follow scientists and engineers through society*, Milton Keynes: Open University Press.

Leslie, C. 1976, "Pluralism and integration in the Indian and Chinese medical systems", In Kleinman, A., Kunstadter, P., Alexander, W. R. & Gale J. S. (eds.) *Medicine in Chinese cultures: comparative studies of health care in Chinese and other societies*, Bethesda: National Institutes of Health, pp. 401–417.

Ley, B. L. 2009, *From pink to green: disease prevention and the environmental breast cancer movement*, New Brunswick: Rutgers University Press.

Luger, T. A., Lahfa, M., Fölster-Holst, R., Gulliver, W. P., Allen, R., Molloy, S., Barbier, N., Paul, C. & Bos, J. D. 2004, "Long-term safety and tolerability of pimecrolimus cream 1% and topical corticosteroids in adults with moderate to severe atopic dermatitis", *Journal of Dermatological Treatment*, vol. 15, no. 3, pp. 169–178.

Matsushige, T. 2010, *Kanjya Chūshin no Iryō toiu Gensetsu: Kanjya no 'Chi' no Shakaigaku (The theory of 'patient-centered medicine': sociology of patient 'knowledge')*, Tokyo: Rikkyo University Press.

McCormic, S. 2009, *No family history: the environmental links to breast cancer*, Lanham: Rowman & Littlefield publishers.

McKevitt, C. 2013, "Experience, knowledge and evidence: a comparison of research relations in health and anthropology", *Evidence and Policy: A Journal of Research, Debate and Practice, The Policy Press, University of Bristol*, vol. 9, no. 1, pp. 113–130.

Ministry of Health, Labour and Welfare. 2014, "Kanjya chōsa: shippei bunrui hen (Patients survey: sorted by diseases)", viewed 21 March 2019, www.mhlw.go.jp/toukei/saikin/hw/kanja/10syoubyo/index.html.

Moynihan, R., Heath, I. & Henry, D. 2002 "Selling sickness: the pharmaceutical industry and disease mongering", *BMJ: British Medical Journal*, vol. 324, no. 7342, pp. 886–891.

Murakami, Y. 2002, "Atarashii ishi kanjya kankei (Doctor-patient relations revisited)", *100-syūnen Kinen Symposium (100th Anniversary Symposium)*, Tokyo: Nihon Igakkai, pp. 6–10.

Muraoka, K. 2000, "Minkan iryō no anatomy (Anatomy of folk medicine)", In Satō, J. (ed.) *Bunka Genshō toshite no Iyashi: Minkan Iryō no Genzai (Healing as a cultural phenomenon: the current status of folk medicine)*, Osaka: Medicus Shuppan, pp. 37–76.

Nakagawa, H. 2005, "Atopīseihifuen chiryō no mokuteki toha nanika" (What is the purpose of atopic dermatitis treatment?), In Nakagawa, H. (ed.) *Atopīseihifuen Chiryō no Jissai: Protopic-Nankō Shiyōhō wo Fukumete (The reality of atopic dermatitis treatment: including the usage of protopic ointment)*, Tokyo: Shindan to Chiryōsha, pp. 1–8.

Namihira, E. 1990, *Yamai to Shi no Bunka: Gendai Iryō no Jinruigaku (The culture of disease and death: anthropology of modern medicine)*, Tokyo: Asahi Shimbunsha.

National Institute for Clinical Excellence. 2004, "Frequency of application of topical corticosteroids for atopic eczema", viewed 21 March 2019, www.nice.org.uk/guidance/Ta81.

*News Station*. 1992, Asahi TV.

O'Connor, B. B. 1995, *Healing traditions: alternative medicine and the health professions*, Philadelphia: University of Pennsylvania Press.

O'donovan, O., Moreira, T. & Howlett, E. 2013, "Tracking transformations in health movement organisations: Alzheimer's disease organisations and their changing 'cause regimes", *Social Movement Studies*, vol. 12, no. 3, pp. 316–334.

Ohnuki-Tierney, E. 1984, *Illness and culture in contemporary Japan: an anthropological view*, Cambridge: Cambridge University Press.

Panofsky, A. 2011, "Generating sociability to drive science: patient advocacy organizations and genetics research", *Social Studies of Science*, vol. 41, no. 1, pp. 31–57.

Pollack, A. 1997, "An itch torments many Japanese, but relief is elusive", *The New York Times*, August 19. viewed 21 March 2019, www.nytimes.com/1997/08/19/science/an-itch-torments-many-japanese-but-relief-is-elusive.html.

Pols, J. 2014, "Knowing patients: turning patient knowledge into science", *Science, Technology, & Human Values*, vol. 39, no. 1, pp. 73–97.

Porter, R. 1989, *Health for sale: quackery in England, 1660–1850*, Manchester: Manchester University Press.

Potter Drug and Chemistry Corporation. 1904, "Eczema: The world's greatest skin humour. Affects every age and condition. The only sure cure is Cuticura", *Essex Newsman*, 9 April, p. 3.

Primary Care Dermatology Society & British Association of Dermatologists. 2009, "Guidelines for the management of atopic eczema", *Skin*, vol. 39, pp. 399–402.

Rapaport, M. J. & Lebwohl, M. 2003, "Corticosteroid addiction and withdrawal in the atopic: the red burning skin syndrome", *Clinics in Dermatology*, vol. 21, no. 3, pp. 201–214.

Satō, J. 2000, "Minkan iryō ni asu wa aruka?: minkan iryō no mirai gaku (Can folk medicine survive?: the future of folk medicine)", In Satō. J. (ed.) *Bunka Genshō toshite no Iyashi: Minkan Iryō no Genzai (Healing as a cultural phenomenon: the current status of folk medicine)*, Osaka: Medicus Shuppan, pp. 285–306.

Satō, K. 2008, *Kanjya ni Mananda Seijingata Atopy Chiryō: Datsu-steroid, Datsu-hoshitsu Ryōhō (Learning how to treat adult atopic dermatitis from patients: steroid/moisture withdrawal treatment)*, Tokyo: Tsuge Shobō Shinsha.

Scottish Intercollegiate Guidelines Network. 2011, "Management of atopic eczema in primary care: a national clinical guideline", viewed 21 March 2019, www.sign.ac.uk/assets/sign125.pdf.

Suetonius. 2017, *The lives of the twelve Caesars complete*, Available at www.amazon.co.uk/kindlestore (Downloaded: 2 September 2017).

Sumiyoshi, J. 1996, *Steroid wo Yameta Riyū: Ridatsu Keikensha 35 nin ni yoru Shōgen (Reasons for stopping steroids: testimony from 35 patients)*, Tokyo: Tsuge Shobō Shinsha.

Suzuki, A. 2010, "Kanjya wo Ikiru: Otona no Atopy" (The lives of patients: adult atopy), *Asahi Shimbun*, 9 November, p. 35, 10 November, p. 33, 11 November, p. 29, 12 November, p. 34, 13 November, p. 33, 14 November, p. 33.

Takehara, K. 2000, *Atopī Business (The atopy business)*, Tokyo: Bungeishunjyū.

Takeuchi, K. & Takenoshita, T. 2009, *Kōhei, Muryō, Kokuei wo Tsuranuku Eikoku no Iryō Kaikaku (Fair, free, and state-run, the UK medical reform)*, Tokyo: Shūeisha.

Tamaki, A. 2008, *Ninin Sankyaku de Naosu Atopy: Chiryō no Saizensen kara (Curing atopy with cooperation: from the frontier of treatment)*, Osaka: Seifūdō Shoten.

Thomas, K., Fall, M., Parry, G. & Nicholl, J. 1995, "National survey of access to complementary health care via general practice", viewed 7 March 2012, www.shef.ac.uk/content/1/c6/07/96/92/MCRU%20access1%201995.pdf.

Tsuge, A. 2004, "'Naosu koto' wo meguru kattō: Sentan iryō no alternative nitsuite kangaeru (The dispute on 'cure': searching for an alternative for advanced medicine)", In Kondo, H. & Ukigaya, S. (eds.) *Gendai Iryō no Minzokushi (An ethnography of contemporary medicine)*, Tokyo: Akashi Shoten, pp. 123–163.

Tsujiuchi, T. 2004, "Post-modern iryō ni okeru modern: hokan daitai iryō no jissen to senmonshokuka (Modern in post-modern medicine: practice and professionalization of complementary and alternative medicine)", In Kondo, H. & Ukigaya, S. (eds.) *Gendai Iryō no Minzokushi (An ethnography of contemporary medicine)*, Tokyo: Akashi Shoten, pp. 183–224.

Tsujiuchi, T., Nakagami, A. & Taniguchi, R. 2009, "Iryō jinruigaku kara mita hokan daitai iryō no sekai" (A medical anthropological perspective of the world of complementary and alternative medicine), *Byōin (Hospital)*, vol. 68, no. 11, pp. 919–923.

Ueda, H. 1998, "Atopīseihifuen ha zōka shitaka (Has the number of atopic dermatitis patients increased?)" In Yoshida, H. (ed.) *Atopīseihifuen (Atopic dermatitis)*, Tokyo: Nippon Hyōronsha, pp. 27–38.

Ueno, C. 2011, *Kea no Shakaigaku: Tōjisha-syuken no Hukushi Shakai he (Sociology of care: toward a patient-centred welfare society)*, Tokyo: Ōta Shuppan.

Ukigaya, S. 2004, *Byōki dakedo Byōki deha nai: Tōnyōbyō to Tomoni Ikiru Seikatu Sekai (Sick but not sick: a life with diabetes)*, Tokyo: Seishin Shobō.

Williams, H. C. 2000, "What is atopic dermatitis and how should it be defined in epidemiological studies?" In Williams, H. C. (ed.) *Atopic dermatitis: the epidemiology, causes, and prevention of atopic eczema*, Cambridge: Cambridge University Press, pp. 3–24.

Williams, H. C., Burney, P. G. J., Pembroke, A. C. & Hay, R. 1994, "The U.K. Working Party's Diagnostic Criteria for Atopic Dermatitis. III. Independent hospital validation", *The British Journal of Dermatology*, vol. 131, pp. 406–416.

Williams, H., Robertson, C., Stewart, A., Aït-Khaled, N., Anabwani, G., Anderson, R., Asher, I., Beasley, R., Björkstén, B., Burr, M., Clayton, T., Crane, J., Ellwood, P., Keil, U., Lai, C., Mallol, J., Martinez, F., Mitchell, E., Montefort, S., Pearce, N., Shah, J., Sibbald, B., Strachan, D., von Mutius, E. & Weiland, S. K. 1999, "Worldwide variations in the prevalence of symptoms of atopic eczema in the international study of asthma and allergies in childhood", *Journal of Allergy and Clinical Immunology*, vol. 103, no. 1, pp. 125–138.

Yamamoto, S. & Kawano, Y. 2006, *Atopīseihifuen Shinryō Guideline 2006 (Guidelines for atopic dermatitis treatment 2006)*, Tokyo: Kyōwa Kikaku.

Zollman, C. & Vickers, A. 1999, "ABC of complementary medicine: complementary medicine and the patient", *BMJ: British Medical Journal*, vol. 319, no. 7223, pp. 1486–1489.

Zwicky, J. F. & American, M. A. 1993, *Reader's guide to alternative health methods*, Chicago: American Medical Association.

# Index

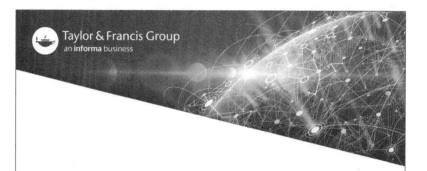

Made in the USA
Las Vegas, NV
26 October 2024

10363898R00090